FIERCE GRACE COLLECTIVE

COLLECTIVE

course book

I dedicate this book to the women
Who chose to find their value from within.
To women who day after day after day say yes
To the love and connection they desire.
To the women who are tired of pretending and pushing through,
I dedicate this to you ::

— Carrie-Anne

GRATITUDE

I AM grateful For:
Guru Singh and GurperKarma Kaur who have guided me
with grace- care and fierce love and the best Yogi
Tea on the planet.

I AM grateful for:
Paramatma Siri Sadhana who with her translation of
the cosmos and this journey of life has mentored me
to step into my excellence.

I AM grateful for:
My mama who has always loved me and that initial
seed of mother love has impacted every part of my
journey.

I AM grateful:
For Steven Roy my husband who has always challenged
me to stretch and who has been one of my greatest
teachers usually at the kitchen table drinking tea.

I AM grateful For:
Sadie Rose Casey who has been my creative partner in
all things Annapurna Living. Sadie You are my rock
and my diamond.

I AM grateful for :
All the artists that through sound uplift and
elevate my life
Snatam Kaur Khalsa, Aykanna, Nirinjan Kaur Khalsa,
Jai, Jagdeesh, Ane Brun, Gurunam Singh, Guru Singh,
Anais Mitchell, Frank Ocean

I AM grateful for:
Celeste Caldwell who supports me and my family with love and her unwavering faith.

I AM grateful for:
My children who are everything to me and who teach me everything.

I AM grateful for:
The women in my immediate circle who surround me with love and friendship.
Mel, Elizabeth, Heike, Malin, Nicole, Maria, Nadine, Emily, Lisa, Lisa, Delaine, Maggie, Natalie, Robyn, Amanda, Krysten, Jessica, Annie, Jesse, Sukhdev, Kelly, Elena, Kathleen, Katie, Maya.

I AM grateful For:
Michelle Gardella whose friendship and artistry inspires every cell of my me.

I AM grateful for:
The teachings of Yogi Bhajan-
I never met him but my dear teachers have shared their experience and love of him with me and I am forever grateful for the incredible teachings of Kundalini Yoga.

I AM grateful for:
The Women of the Fierce Grace Collective. You women have touched my soul so deeply and I truly bow to each of you.

I AM grateful for
This breath and this breath and this one too.

TABLE OF CONTENTS

INTRODUCTION

Welcome to The Fierce Grace Collective.

Here is the dance we do here:

We ground.
We quiet.
We ask ourselves, "What wants to come through me?"

We make Intentions ::
We place these wishes/ intentions at the altar of
our lives.
We add some energy, movement, and action.
We add nourishment and gratitude.

Inhale nourish
Exhale fear
Inhale love
Exhale fear

We move through the days, the months, the moments
with our hearts open,
Listening to the inner voice that whispers what we
need.
She screams sometimes too.

We look to what's in front of us to teach us.
We look to our lives to teach us.
We protect what we love.

We create what we love.

We release.
We let go of what just isn't working.
We release.
And then we do it all over again.
We repeat.

Each month is different and the structure gives us
scaffolding that holds us up when we need support.

We catch a glimpse of our living altars and feel
taken care of.
We look at the mundane moments—the setting-the-
table, the making-the-tea, the long drive to work—as
the art that makes our lives.

We don't wait for things to change.
We create the change,
within.

I welcome you to this experience with all my heart.

Together:
We will strengthen, we will nourish,
we will examine and self-enquire;
We will flourish through thought and action.
We will radiate and glow from within.

Be gentle with yourself, go at your own pace.
Feel worthy.
Be true to yourself.
Love so fiercely and purely that the gaze of love you
have for your life brings tears to your heart.

I ache for this.
I ache for connection.

Your life is here.
Your life is now.
Bring all of yourself to it.

I welcome you, I welcome you, I welcome you.

Love,
Carrie-Anne

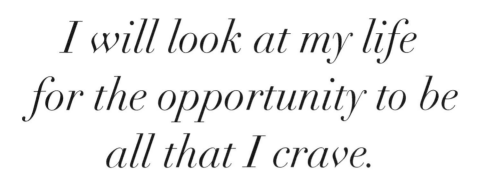

I will look at my life
for the opportunity to be
all that I crave.

I will share with others
and open my heart.

TUNING IN

We begin every session by tuning in.
To tune in, chant three times:

ONG NAMO GURU DEV NAMO

This means "I bow to the divine teacher within and all the divine
teachers who have come before me"

For an extended tuning in, we then chant:

AAD GURAY NAMEH
JUGAAD GURAY NAMEH
SAT GURAY NAMEH
SIRI GURU DAYVAY NAMEH

This translates as:
I bow to the primal wisdom
I bow to the wisdom true through the ages
I bow to the true wisdom
I bow to the great unseen wisdom

When we close, we sing:

MAY THE LONG TIME SUN SHINE UPON YOU
ALL LOVE SURROUND YOU
AND THE PURE LIGHT WITHIN YOU
GUIDE YOUR WAY HOME

FIVE SUTRAS OF THE AQUARIAN AGE

BY

YOGI BHAJAN

RECOGNIZE THAT THE OTHER PERSON IS YOU

THERE IS A WAY THROUGH EVERY BLOCK

WHEN THE TIME IS ON YOU, START, AND THE PRESSURE WILL BE OFF

UNDERSTAND THROUGH COMPASSION OR YOU WILL MISUNDERSTAND THE TIMES

VIBRATE THE COSMOS, AND THE COSMOS SHALL CLEAR THE PATH

A BIT ABOUT THE MOON

The **New Moon** is viewed as the beginning of the cycle. It is when you can't see the moon in the sky at all. This phase is associated with new beginnings, planting the seeds, and setting intentions. In this Collective, we talk about New Moon rituals, which always include: tending to the altar. Setting intentions and writing them down.

The **Full Moon** is the fullest point of the moon cycle, when you can see the entire thing in the sky. It is associated with fertility and creativity, and the feeling of wrapping things up, harvesting, etc. In this Collective, we talk about Full Moon rituals, which include releasing your fears, burdens, and attachments. Dancing it out. Resting. Going inward.

The **Waxing Moon** is when the moon is going from New to Full, so from nothing to something. Think growth, gathering, expansion.

The **Waning Moon** is when the moon is going from Full to New, so it's getting smaller and fading. Think letting go, freedom, compost, self-care.

Of course, all of these are just guides. As you tune in, you will notice your own themes and patterns and begin to create your own rituals. Always listen to yourself and your own body above all else.

New Moon

Waning Moon

Waxing Moon

Full Moon

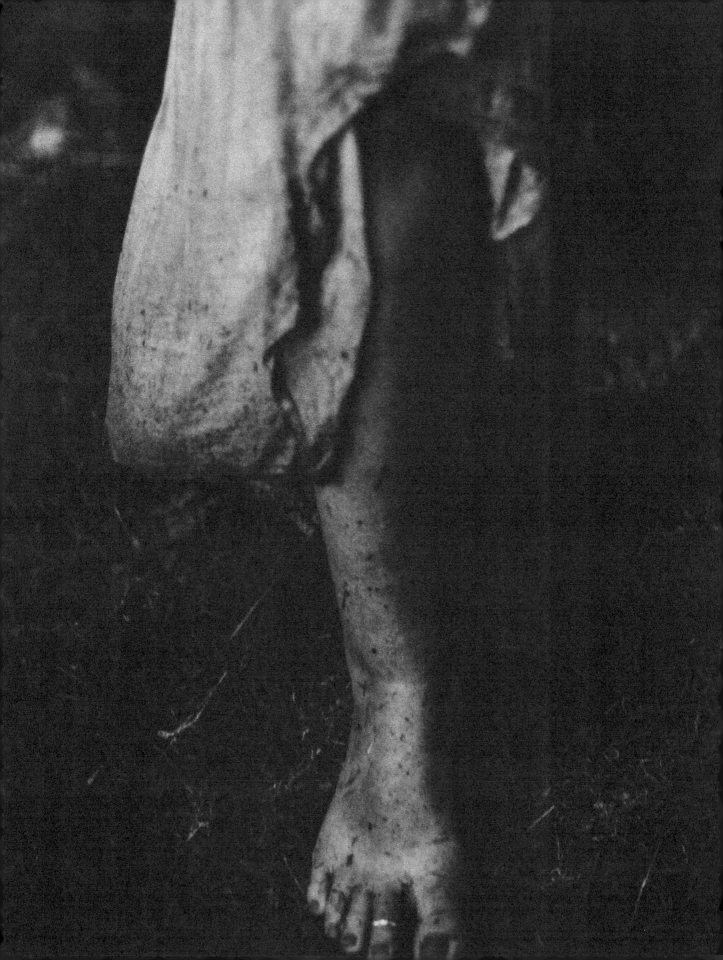

ROOTING IN

ROOTING IN

To ground,
To be steady,
To feel supported,
To find strength from within.
To feel and be supported so that when I get triggered
by my stuff, my foundation holds me up.
It keeps me steady.
My foundation reminds me of who I am.
I remember who I am.
I am not my feelings.
My feelings are the canary in the coal mine—the
flashing light in my car that reminds me I need to
refuel.
The blow-up in the kitchen is not about the thing
I'm screaming about, but about the tears underneath
it.

I am not my feelings,
but they are indicators, secret messages, reminders
of what I need.
They are the way through the block.
They are showing me where the block is.
Perhaps it's loneliness.
Perhaps I'm hungry.
Perhaps I need to weed out some extra weight that is
holding me down.
With a strong foundation, I can explore what's up
without falling apart so badly that I can't get up.

When my foundation is strong and true,
I can weather the storms.
I can keep on keeping up.
I can create,
I can love,

I can be clear,
I can be true to what I believe,
I can be kind.

I am not calm and stoic all the time
(of course I'm not)
I am, however, able to catch myself when I get hooked
and find a way to rise above.

My practice,
My foundation
Gives me this.

This is freedom for me::
In the quiet of the morning, I sit in the space of my
soul and I connect to my inner wisdom and the great
wisdom that is there for me.

It's there for you, too.
We just need to get quiet enough to hear it.
Even in this noisy world that tells us all day long
that there is more to want and more to be.
It's a world that doesn't truly value the feminine
and so we must teach ourselves to value it; and
then we must pass that value on through example and
inspiration and expression.

When I sit in the quiet and start my day with
reverence,
I greatly shift the experience of my life.
From this shift
Anything is possible....

ROOTING IN

We are here to transform and elevate our lives. This is just the beginning. We begin with settling in and getting to know ourselves.

When we are rooted in ourselves, we are grounded and able to take care of our basic needs and feel comfortable in our bodies. When we are unbalanced at the root, we can be fearful and insecure and life feels like a burden. We feel we don't belong anywhere. Our constitution is weak. We have limited physical and mental strength.

By doing exercises and meditations that root us in, we can shift out of this dissatisfying state easily and gracefully. Carrying around the burden of discomfort and insecurity is draining, and not only that—it's unnecessary! Do you ever have those days where it's easy to not care what other people think? Let's have more of those days. Nothing's ever perfect, but we can exercise spiritual muscles that get us closer to our ideal.

The theme for this chapter is simplicity and nourishment. Being rooted is simple, but it is not always easy. In fact, simplicity is very difficult in this day and age.

For this journey, I invite you to create an altar space. You'll be amazed how an altar assists you in rooting in. Creating a sacred space affects you even wehn the size of your altar is small. If all you have room for is a candle on your bedside table; do it. You will thank yourself for it. An altar doesn't need be grand, it just needs to be.

Altars and meditation are two primary tools that help me feel rooted. But these are not the only tools. Breathing, slowing down, drinking tea, taking a bath. These are all things that ground us. Another thing that helps is other women. Women need other women. We need to confide in each other, laugh with each other, reflect with each other, gather and connect.

You are not alone.

Build your altar

Create a sacred space for yourself.

If you already have an altar, take this opportunity to clean it and infuse new energy into it. Does it need to be dusted off? Sprayed with rosewater? Do your treasures need to spend a day in the sun or a night in the moonlight? Tune into your space and ask it what it needs. If you don't have a space yet, you're in for a treat. First time altars are super special. First, find a place for your altar. This can sometimes be tricky and you may need to be clever. It's not always obvious right away. If you have a toddler, your altar may be best high off the ground. I love having mine close to the ground so I can sit by it.

Which place speaks to you? When you find it, claim it. As you seek and find the space, hold an intention that you will meditate here daily, (with flexibility of course). This space will feel different after a month of attention. You will raise the vibration of the space with your attention here. Remember, keep it simple.

After you set up your space, sit by the altar. Light a candle and breathe for a bit. Do your meditations here. This is the place where you will root in. Come here to remember yourself.

About Altars

A new moon is the perfect time to revisit, adjust, and clean your altar space. Each month during the new moon, I tend to my altar space and I encourage you to do the same. Freshen it up. See what wants to come down or what new things might want to be added.

Your altar space does not need to be fancy or grand, it can be simple and small or humble. It can have flowers or crystals or just a candle and your favorite book, a love letter to yourself, a drawing from your child. Whatever brings you peace, place it there.

If you don't have an altar as part of your home or practice, I encourage you to set one up, as I refer to altars often in this book. I have known women to get incredibly creative with setting up their altars: on dressers, on bedside tables, and I know one woman who even set hers up on the back of the door, just by hanging things that brought her the feeling of peace. Your altar can be anywhere.

My altar is on a windowsill in my kitchen, and I love looking at it day in and day out. It soothes me.

Build your altar. Let it be your anchor while reading this book and through your days. Take the next new moon to dust it off and give it some love. Let it soothe your heart.

Love,
Carrie-Anne

NEW MOON INTENTIONS

Note: This was designed for a new moon week. The new moon is when the moon is not illuminated and cannot be seen from Earth because it is aligned between the sun and the earth with its dark side facing the Earth. You can use these practices for any new moon cycle, or any time you wish, no matter where the moon is.

The New Moon is a guide and a wise friend. It's a powerful time to set intentions. The new moon opens a portal for us every 28 days. We always have access to the moon's magic, and when we pay attention to the phases we bring simple much-needed ritual to our lives for women, this is a sacred gift.

For me, it's important to have an awareness of the Lunar Calendar and to keep an eye on it so that I know what is going on. The moon rules us women. It rules the ocean tides. It is not to be taken lightly.

In the last chapter I asked you to build an altar so that you'd have your own space for peace and meditation. Now let's look at intentions. On the new moon, plant the seeds of intention that you will tend to by metaphorically watering, weeding and caring for them.

What are your intentions? Bring them to your altar. Sing them while you do the dishes. Delight in them as you drive to work. Let them be wild or crazy, simple or gentle. Whatever they may be, let them be alive.

Hopefully you are beginning to create a gentle flow at your altar with your meditation or breathing. Even one minute a day is amazing. The centering and inner-work will help you root into yourself. With time, clear answers will flow through you as you meditate. You'll learn to listen.

Writing your intentions

Write out your intentions and wishes. I want you to get real with yourself. What do you want to create this year? This week? Make it something that turns you on and stirs you up. Get clear about it. Write freely about it. Let your come out of the depths where it has been hiding. What does it look like? What does it feel like? Sometimes it feels uncomfortable to write what we want, but that's where the power lies. Keep the letter at your altar, or anywhere that feels best to you. Revisit it often.

Here is my letter of intentions which I keep under my mattress and re-read whenever I want. I add to it on each new moon until I feel ready to start anew. I write mine out by hand and I am grateful for this opportunity to be aligned with the moon and the power she gives me in my life.

My Intentions

Dear Moon,

Today I see my life as an outpouring of my thoughts, so I discipline my mind with thoughts that support my vision to create a business that has the potential to change the world through nourishment and connection to self.

I embrace that all of this is possible for me and my vision.
I align with others who feel this calling knowing that as a collective we have more power.
I support my family in their uniqueness, letting go of any judgement I have.
I am open to friendships that elevate and make me laugh.
I am open to the magic that will bring awareness and great revelations to what I am doing.
My business grows and I work with ease and joy. I support those around me

WEEDING THE GARDEN

It's time to take a look at the places where we maybe stuck and at the things that don't work. This may be hard and uncomfortable, but the discomfort is where the growth is. There are no shortcuts here, only true intention, action and nourishment. I encourage you to stretch yourself and to tune into your own divine wisdom. Take your time. If one of these prompts ever brings up something for you that is too much, just move on and revisit it another time.

Imagine your life is a garden. You till the soil and plant your seeds. You water it, maybe even feed the soil with nutrients. You make sure things are getting enough sun or shade, and you tend the garden each day to make sure it has everything it needs. You give so much to this garden and to each plant so that it may grow.

But there's something else. You have to remove things too to make space for what you've planted. You pull weeds, remove snails, clear debris. Some weeds appear without your notice. One day it suddenly seems like they've taken over, and you spend hours pulling them out gently so that they don't disrupt the roots of your plants. Pulling things out of your garden ends up being just as important as putting things in. If we don't pull things out, our garden ends up full of things we never even wanted there in the first place.

This happens in our life, too. It is to our benefit to check into our lives daily, to see if weeds are growing. Weeds show up as obligations that don't serve us, relationships that drain us, commitments that are no longer healthy, routines that need to be shifted, and so on. It's hard to recognize these things. It takes careful attention and practice and it also takes courageous action to remove them. Meditation is a helpful tool for this. As you create quiet space in your mind, it becomes more and more clear what is not serving your bliss. Over time, you will gather courage to remove those weeds in your life.

Noticing the weeds is the first step. Pulling them out is the hardest part: changing routines is not easy, and if there is a person who is a weed, that can be even more difficult. But, if there's one thing I do know, it's that setting boundaries around ourselves gives us incredible fortitude and strength.

Holding true to our needs is essential, even if it means hurting someone's feelings or letting go of a commitment that we wish we loved but that we just don't.

Now that you have your altar space and your list of intentions, your garden space is looking pretty fresh, isn't it? It's like you've tilled the earth and selected your seeds and everything is ready to happen. This is the perfect moment for you to find out what doesn't belong in your garden, what doesn't nourish your soil. Keep your list of intentions close by as you go through the worksheet on the next page. Your list will remind you of what you really want.

Remember, be selfish in these exercises. Even if you "want to want" something because it would make a loved-one happy, if it isn't quite what you want, that's okay. The truth shall set you free.

You don't have to decide all of this in one sitting. Each day, notice what you love and what you don't. Listen to yourself if you're groaning about a commitment or obligation. Noticing is powerful and being at peace with what you notice is even more powerful. Don't resist your true feelings. If you do, the feeling will keep returning until you look at it.

There is great power in setting intentions, creating a disciplined yoga and meditation practice, and creating the life you desire. I honor you and your dedication and I encourage you to nourish yourself through not only what you eat and do, but through what you think and decide.

Know that you are divine and that your birthright is majestic.

Who would I be if...

Go for a walk around your neighborhood or a hike, a stroll at the beach. Whatever you have near you, do that. As you walk, think about who you would be if you were connected to yourself and your center. If you were deeply rooted, who would you be?

Ask yourself where you are deeply rooted and where your strengths lie. Also ask yourself where you don't feel rooted, where you feel vulnerable, frustrated or scattered. Consider these questions: "If I were centered and grounded and myself, *What might I let go of? What might I do more of?*

An example from my life: If I were centered and grounded...

I would walk more, everyday (without my phone) just to move my body and take in whatever nature I can. I would be calmer. I wouldn't react as much. I wouldn't yell and scream when my buttons are pushed. As for what I could let go of? Well, there's a texting relationship with a friend that tends to take up a lot of my time, yet doesn't move either of us anywhere. It's a distraction from what I truly need to do and I don't like that, it doesn't nourish me. I'd also organize my day in such a way that I have lots of space to BE and also make space for the tasks that really do improve my life like meditation, yoga, going for a walk and making healthy food. As simple as that sounds, those are big goals!

Ask yourself this question everyday if you want. Even if it's during a 5 minute walk or in the bathtub. Put your hands on your tummy and take a deep breath in and ask, "Who would I be?"

Daydream a little bit, explore it. Nothing is out of reach.

CELEBRATE THE FULL MOON

To me, the moon cycle means opportunity for ritual. Now I'm not talking long white dresses and wild bonfire rituals. My truth is that I'm a busy mother and a householder and as it is now, wild nature rituals don't fit easily in my life. And that's okay. I bring ritual in to my days other ways. Sometimes for the full moon, I dance for fifty-two minutes. I encourage you to use this ritual (or one of your own!) to celebrate the full moon and to honor its cycle with your own. Keep it simple, there is no need for pressure. Ritual doesn't have to be grand.

This is important work, but it doesn't have to be hard. Pay attention to where resistance is coming from and then don't dwell there for too long. Discipline is important, but so is joy.

Spiritual success comes from a delicate balance of these two things; discipline and joy. If you are not feeling calm and peaceful and enlightened that's okay! Let it be.

Sometimes we need to remove ourselves from "the trying" altogether in order for things to flow as they are intended to.

*Many blessings on
your full heart.*

Observe the light

Sometime today, notice where the light falls around your home or office or in your car. Even on the grayest of mornings you will find brightness tucked into a corner or resting on the edge of a leaf.

When you catch that light, take a deep breath and feel the earth beneath your feet. At some point today, write three things that you know are true.

The truth is…

The truth is…

The truth is…

Revel in the progress made here. Treat yourself. Kiss someone you love. Bathe. Walk. Breathe.

Weeding the Garden

In order to keep the garden of our life healthy and blooming, we have to make sure it doesn't become overgrown with weeds. This can be a delicate process. First, we must determine what should stay and what should go. This takes a peaceful observation, a knowing and noticing. Then we have to actually remove the weeds. This takes devotion and work, getting our hands dirty, and good old-fashioned determination.

Let's start figuring it out.

Write a list of things that you do in your daily life that seem mundane.
This may include chores, driving. Cooking, dishes, cleaning, reading
books to kiddos at night, making breakfast ... these types of things.

✎ ...

Write a list of things that you do socially or for your own benefit.

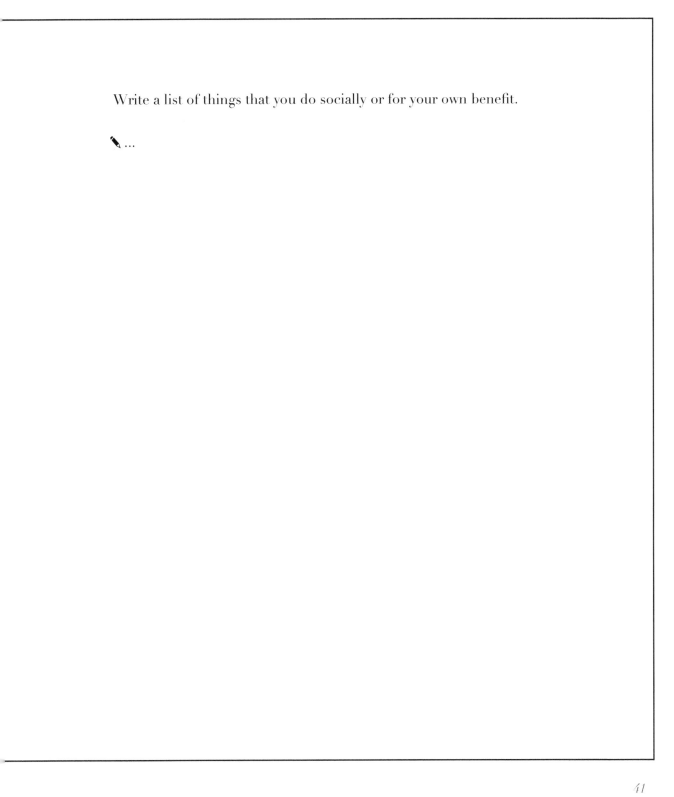 ...

Make a list of ways that you pass your time like habits or things you do with your down time. These can include reading, social media, listening to music, chatting with your friends or partner. If you spend time on your device spacing out, that counts! Write it all down. Time is an important currency.

 ...

Now go back into your lists and circle the things in each of these sections that you LOVE. If there isn't one that you love, that's fine. Don't circle anything. Take the circled items and write them here:

✎ ...

With a different colored pen, go back through the list and circle the things you actually really don't like. These are things you look at and they don't lift you up when you read them on the list. Notice how your body feels when you look through the items on your lists. Write those circles things here:

✎ …

These two refined lists are imporant. In one, you have the things you love to do. In another, you have the things you really don't love to do. Look at the list of things you don't love. What can shift? Can any of these be eliminated from your life? How? Can some of them be reduced? Delegated? Changed in some way? This will take some creativity, thought and intention.

Brainstorm here about replacements or ways you can unload
the things you don't love. Make a list of things that need to be
communicated in order to make these changes. Start with one thing.
Who will you need to call? To whom will you need to express your true
feelings? Who might be disappointed by these changes? Write it all
down, even if you aren't looking forward to it.

✎ ...

\Finally, go back and look at the list of things you LOVE. Can you cultivate more of these things? Take them to the next level? Share them in more ways? Brainstorm here about ways to bring more of what you love into your life and garden.

✎ ...

Congratulations! This is a lot of work you have done here. Now for the last thing. Write down the very first task you will do to begin pulling weeds from your life. Be specific. Write down the day and the task, just like anything else you'd put in your planner. And yes, put it in your planner.

 ...

Let the change begin.

Journal

Journal

DANCE
OF THE POET

DANCE OF THE POET

Creativity is the gateway to the life I want.
I am an artist.
I didn't always feel like one, but when I embraced
that yes I am an artist, my life started to shift.
We are all artists.
We are always creating.
We are always giving birth
To ideas,
To new ways,
To gardens (metaphorical and real).
I am an artist when I creatively tend to my loves.
I am an artist when I boil water for tea.
I am an artist when I look my kid in the eyes and
tell him how I feel and ask what's up with him.

My husband reads a lot of deep spiritual text. He's
a hardy New England soul and not fluffy in any way.
One afternoon he shared with me and our little girl
and our beloved Celeste who helps us at home about
part of meditation that he was exploring. We all sat
on the floor in the kitchen and he led us through
the mediation. We chanted, we whispered, then we
mentally chanted and then he said, "now listen for
the sound."
Wow.
Listen for the sound::

What is the sound of your life?
Throughout your day, take the time to listen to your
life.

You are the writer, the director, the producer, and
the star of your life.
You create the life you want by the choices you make
and the actions you take.

Life will challenge us.
Be an artist.
Be creative, and simple things will feel divine.

Be a poet and a dancer and bring all of your body,
your soul, and your being to your glorious life one
breath at at time....

You are the poet. You get to write it.

AWARENESS OF SONG

Too often we move through life forgetting that in each moment we get to create our present. It's easy to let the sameness of routine cloud the day in a way that doesn't allow us to to see and celebrate the wild beauty of being here on earth. Just as we're tied to the cycles of the moon, so we are tied to the cycles of the season. Mother nature is always, regenerating, quietly displaying her charms for our amazement. Likewise, we are awakening and regenerating, slowly unfurling the beauty within as we tenderly remember what it's like to be in the light.

As a woman you're a creator. You are the poet in a constant dance with life. With every movement, word, thought, and soul-song you are weaving together the ordinary beauty that is life. To embrace the body of the poet is to simply choose to see the magic in your ordinary day. It is to breathe, notice, and revere. It is to bring awareness to your own song, the song you sing each moment, the vibration you carry with you everywhere you go.

Bringing awareness to your own uniqueness involves a simultaneous awareness of your inner self and your outer self. It involves taking responsibility for who you are in each moment. For me, this is a recurring theme. I think to myself "It is not *what* do I want to be, but *who* I want to be."

Who do you want to be? How can you become this? Are you already who you want to be? Our circumstances do not define us. Our job does not define us. What is in our hearts defines us. The actions we take each day define us.

Don't sweat the small things. As we learn to release these small hindrances, we are able to be more fully ourselves, more fully open, more receptive, and also more giving. What are your desires? Let them in. Do not be afraid. Let them fill your body and heart, let yourself see them in their fullness. Let yourself be deserving of them.

Allow yourself to simmer in your uniqueness. Whatever it is, it is your gift. You are perfect just the way you are. It is your particular you-ness that draws people in, brings you what you need, sings your song to your angels. Let it be. How do we let ourselves be? It is a practice, a daily devotion. We allow the good, the bad and the ugly. We allow the pain and the pleasure.

In quiet moments remember to breathe. If there is anything certain, it is that the flowers will once again bloom. You are just another expression of Mother Nature, another facet of her perfect geometry. Become acutely aware of your body and the messages it sends. What is unfurling in you right now? How does it align to what's around you? What is showing up inside your heart and inside your home?

Poetry

The first rays of light that appear as the moon waves goodbye.

The arch in your back as you stretch into the new day.

The thud of small feet making their way towards you.

The way your hand guides the knife as you slice through carrots and onions and celery.

The lips that touch your cheek as you tuck them into bed.

This is the poetry of life.

Today, pay special attention to the world around you and all the tiny magical ways you move within it. Write it down as you go through the day. Make sure to capture the smells, the sounds and the feelings you experience as you flow through the day. Discover the everyday miracles that lay at your feet. Before you go to bed, take some time to write a full page in your journal. Use the notes that you took. Look over them. What stands out at you? Did it help you to notice more simple beauty?

If you are feeling brave, write a poem about your day. It can be sad, joyful, simple, easy, intricate. Writing poetry can make us feel vulnerable but it can teach us a lot about the power of simple beauty.

CONNECTING TO THE WISH

Remember to tend to your altar this month. An altar is a living thing, just like you … keep it reflecting you. It can be helpful to revisit. Look at it. Ask what it needs. Does anything need to be added? Removed? Does it need to be dusted, blessed, given flowers? Our altars anchor us in so many ways. Tend to it, and in doing so, tend to yourself.

What is your wish? For many of us, there is a wish to "be" something: a photographer, a writer, a painter, a yogini, and so on. Big dreams, small dreams, so many dreams. For some women, the wish is to live somewhere else, perhaps where life would be slower (or faster), or to travel. Perhaps the wish is to have more family, or to have an art show at a gallery. Whatever it is, it's your wish. It belongs to you, and it has things to tell you.

Do you know what your wish is? Wishes often get buried by everyday life. I believe we all have a wish. A wish can be as simple as just being present with yourselves or with your family.

Once you know what your wish is, you get to begin the next phase of discovery. All wishes have a source, and it is the journey back to this source that empowers you, emboldens you and teaches you about yourself and your path. Let's say you want to publish a book about your childhood. This might mean you want to be a writer, or maybe not. Maybe you just want to write that one book because you want to share that story. Take a look at that story. What does it mean to you?

Why do you want to share it? This is important. I believe we all have a story to share. Do you want to help others can learn something that you learned the hard way? Do you want to reach someone who shares part of your story so they won't feel alone, as you might have?

These questions are all part of the journey back to the source.

Along the way you'll learn things. The source may be something entirely different than you imagined.

Let's say you want to be a singer/songwriter. On the path back to source you discover that there is an emotion that lives in your very center, in your belly. It moves through you when you sing, and you feel healed every time you do it. By writing songs and singing, you become a conduit for your own story and emotion, and it is this feeling that you are craving.

As we travel back to source from our wish, we are distilling it to its simplest form. Often, you will find love on this journey. The simplicity leads to love. There is so much love at the source of things.

Find your light

The other day, I walked through the woods with my husband and with a forest ranger who showed us around. As we walked, he told us which trees were healthy and which were not. He used some key words while describing the best environment for healthy trees, such as 'nutrient rich' which stuck out to me. He shared how trees surrounding a certain tree affected the growth of that tree. Sometimes the least healthy ones take up the space and force the other trees to dwarf themselves and then they cannot thrive.

Nature reflects us, of course. Who are the trees surrounding you? Do you dwarf in the presence of someone? Is there a story that keeps you small? Can you let it go? Can you stand up tall with your shoulders back, your heart up and to the light?

Imagine yourself as the tree. Become the tree in your mind. Look around you. Is there light coming in? Is anything blocking your light? Are you having to reach for it, or is it shining easily on all your branches?

Write about your tree vision. Where are your nutrients coming from?

SOFTENING WITH DISCIPLINE

Through discipline, we soften our load. Discipline makes things easier. Weird, right? It seems counterintuitive at first because discipline seems like a struggle, or rigid.

But true discipline is marvelous mastery of the self. It means you know your NO and your YES and you know when to use them. It means you have boundaries for yourself, which means everything else flows through with ease and grace.

First of all, what does discipline mean to you? What is your relationship with it? I've read a lot about discipline. I've read about it in regards to my meditation practice, in regards to parenting and in regards to acting. Discipline manifests in many ways. I think one problem is that discipline gets confused for rules or not having fun. Rules are external, while discipline is internal. Discipline comes from the same source that our wish comes from. It comes from a place of **fluid** strength, not rigidity.

Think of water. The river flows around anything in its way, yet it always flows. Though water is not solid, it still carves canyons and canals, and it can move rock from millions of years ago. It is this kind of softness that allows us to be ourselves.

It is flowing around the obstacles, following our true path no matter what's in the way.

When we are tempted to stress out or to feel like we aren't getting enough done for ourselves, this is when softness is the most valuable. When we are soft, we can change, we can flow.

Softening

In spring, the ice that caps the mountains begins to melt and the rains begin to fall. The ground softens and the greens and pinks and whites crawl up from the muddy soil. Without the right amount of water, nothing can live — not only what sprouts from the earth beneath our feet but also all of the seeds of life that rest within us. Water is the source of our creativity. It's the life force behind your poetry, your music, your dance, your cooking, your movement ... whatever it is that calls to your creative spirit.

To fully embody our creativity and honor that creative spirit, we must do everything in our power to allow our river to flow and to be free. This is a call to softness. It is a time to soften, to let things be. Being soft means loving yourself, it means showing those negative voices the door, kindly but firmly.

In your journal, write down what comes up for you around these questions:

How can I soften? What does softness mean to me?
Where am I already soft?

RELEASE AND RECEIVING

Who would I be if I let go of the masks I wear? If I let go of my attachments to the roles I play in life? How can I release the wishes I have within my heart? How do I let go while also keeping the faith?

There are moments where I feel my identity slipping away — both as an actress, the profession I love and chose as a young girl, and myself as a mother. Not because I don't want to be an actress, but because I know who I am is not only this. Surrendering the labels I use to myself, the closer I get to my true self.

The mother, the wife, the daughter, the friend … these are all roles I cherish, but at the core of me is my soul: my soul is not an actress or a mother or a wife. My soul is clear and true and not attached to any labels. My soul just IS. What a moment of breakthrough to know that I am not what I do. I can still love what I do and work hard and purely, but in my soul I am free.

Honestly, I still grasp for the attachments — of course I do, I'm a human being. But in the moments that I feel this beauty in my soul and this freedom, I cherish that I have access to this feeling at all. This is why I love meditation so much. Meditation allows me glimpses of this freedom. I want to desire and to create. I am not cutting myself off from these parts of me. Carrie-Anne the actress, the mother, the daughter, the wife, the teacher. I hold them all with respect and awe.

At the same time, I work to access my essence. his is a vital part of my expansion; it is a vital part of my dance with life.

When I dance in my living room on the next full moon, I will dance for the girl in me who had so many dreams. I will dance for the woman who knows the grace of being enough without awards, accolades, or approval from the outside. I will hold that girl with my woman self and tell her I love her so.

HOW DO YOU WANT TO FEEL?

This is a time for throwing your head back into the sun and remembering how you were as a child, all full of wonder and daydreams.

Can you imagine how radically different your life would be if you allowed yourself to sit inside your dreams? If you danced down the rabbit hole of desires? There is is no right or wrong way to dream. There is no right or wrong desire. Anything you dream and desire is worthy of your attention and worthy of you. Remember that your dreams are an indicator of your true essence. You are not your work, you are not your roles. You are simply YOU.

This creative prompt can be done alone, or if you want to gather some girlfriends (or your kids!) to do it with you, it's even more fun. Carve out some time to really sit down for this one.

What you need:
>   Journal and pen
>   Large piece of paper (cardstock or poster board preferred)
>   Pen or Marker
>   A stack of magazines for cutting up images
>   Glue stick or tape
>   Other embellishments

Take your piece of paper (a regular piece is fine, or a larger one if you have it) and draw a line down the middle. Somewhere on the left side, write "What I Want," and on the right side, "How I Want to Feel."

Sort through your magazines and collected images and begin to paste on your board in the appropriate spaces. Let your intuition guide you through this process. You may be surprised at what appears. Once you've finished creating your board, take some time to really absorb it. What colors are repeating? What images really stand out to you? Are there words that are singing to your spirit?

Take your journal and now put into words the images you have collected. Embrace whatever emerges as you let the words flow through you. What do you want? What do you feel when you look at your board? How will your life be different if you allow yourself to step into your desires and feelings?

Distilling

What is your wish? Write down one big wish you have. (If you want to do multiple wishes, copy pages of this worksheet and use one for each wish.) A wish is a dream or vision or life goal.

✎ ...

What emotions and states of being do you hope to feel from this wish? When you imagine this wish coming true, how do you think you will feel because of it?

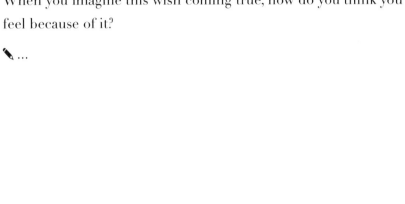 ...

Look at the list of emotions and states of being you just wrote. What are some small, simple ways that you can cultivate these in your daily life, starting now? Where do they show up already that they could be enhanced?

✎ ...

How does your wish embody service? If your wish comes true, how will you then be in service to others?

✎ ...

Look at the list above of ways you will be in service when you live your wish. Are there similar ways that you can be in service, starting now? Anything small and simple is perfect. How can you start to incorporate this service into your daily life?

If I achieve my wish, I will have.....

 ...

Write down the things you think you will have when you are living your wish: success, happiness, money, time... anything that comes to mind. Let the words flow. Write down whatever comes to mind.

✎ ...

Look at the previous list. Do you already have some of these things? Write them down. These things are already serving you and showing you abundance. Practice gratitude and sharing with these things.

✎ ...

Which ones do you feel like you don't have? Write about them and why you want them. Again, consider small, simple ways you can begin to cultivate these things in your daily life.

✎ ...

Journal

Journal

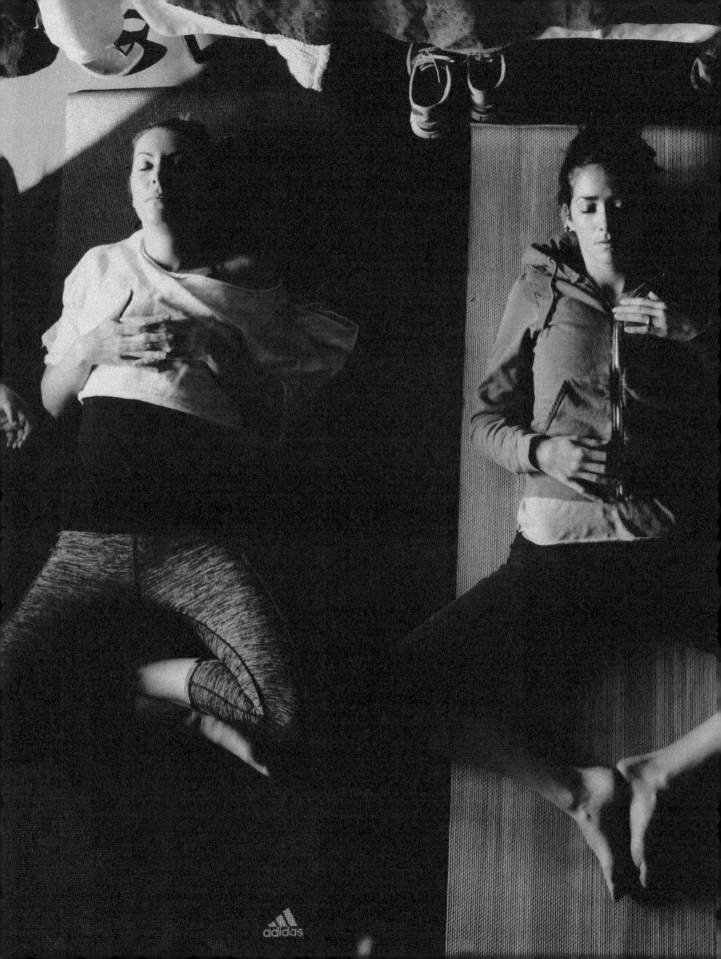

TEMPLE BODY

TEMPLE BODY

Dear Me,
I honor you for always wanting to grow and stretch.
I honor you for the places that are hard to trust.
I honor that there are times you feel afraid and you hold on too tightly.

Dear Me,
I see your perfection and the way you love others so much.
I see the way you care about people you don't even know.
I see the way you feel when there is unkindness in the air.

Dear Me,
I care about you.
I care about the way you feel.
I care about the way you move.

Dear Me,
I promise to love you no matter what.
I promise to be there for you always.
I promise to never abandon you.

Dear Me,
I wish for you to feel all that you are.
I wish that your life expands and that you feel the magic all around you.
I wish that your creativity lights the way for you and others.

Dear Me,
I love you.

There are times when rituals truly hold us up. They hold us together, they tie us to the structure of our life. They guide us when we have nothing left.

STRONG CENTER, SOFT HEART

Navel Center Definition

With a strong navel, we have the ability to stay centered within ourselves. An activated navel gives us stamina and motivation to commit to do what we need to do and to take action when needed to. It helps us say what we mean. When our navel center is weak or out of balance, we feel unmotivated. The navel is your center. The navel is an anchor point, a pivot point from which all action is birthed. When the anchor is strong, we feel free.

Here are some qualities of an underdeveloped naval.

When our navel centers are underdeveloped we can feel:
- Me, only me
- What can I get ?
- ME ME ME
- Power, control
- Win/ loss thinking
- Lack of integrity

When our navel centers are developed we can feel:
- Us, connected to others
- Respect for right action
- Win/ win thinking
- Integrity :: competence for your passion.

A strong navel gives us more than a flat stomach. The navel is a source of power and when it is strong, we are in control of our life. Confidence and certainty abound, and we are in tune with our "gut instincts," an indication of healthy intuition. Having a strong center comes from having a strong practice of attention to self and to intuition. This is why I so very much recommend meditation for this particular aspect. It helps strengthen and attune that which is otherwise hard to understand.

Through our work in this book, we are creating an internal power source to execute the dreams we have in our life.

Being strong in our centers is a way you can be present in your life. It is how we can set boundaries with grace. In this way, you begin to create a life we truly love. This benefits you, your families and the people around you. When you are strong, you allow others to be strong. When you are authentic, you give space for others to be authentic. I often think, "How do I teach the kids these skills?" And I realize it starts with me.

I watch my little one and I see her confidence and I think, "how can I support her to grow and to not be brought down by the dominant culture?" And I know completely. It is only through healing myself and being the fierce nourisher of myself that I can teach her that. I must lead by example. That is the only way. It is my insistence to change the conversation I have with every woman I know and the conversation that I have with myself.

Confidence, joy, and intuition come from the body by anchoring firmly in our centers. It is beneficial to start becoming hyper-aware of your body and how it reacts to situations. Notice the change in your body when you enter a new place, a new building or a new room. There are messages in these reactions. Notice how your body feels when a certain person is speaking to you, or when you engage in certain types of conversation, or when you go outside in the sunshine. These are all indicators, communications from body to spirit. When you pay attention, you learn what each feeling is trying to say to you.

When you listen to your body and feel strong in your center, we emanate a subtle strength that makes us, and those around us, feel safe. And when we feel strong and safe, we move and live differently. We don't think, "How do I look?" But instead we think, "How do I feel?"

I choose to smile at the imperfections of it all.

I choose to stay flexible to the needs of my family.

I choose to ask for help when I need it, knowing that in the act of asking, I am finding a quiet strength.

Return to your center

As women, we thrive on being connected to our feminine energy. We need to be in constant communication with our senses because we are sensual beings. Every inch of our bodies contains so much knowing.

We will always be pulled to forces outside of ourselves, but the key is to remember and develop the ways we can find our way back to our true north; our center. What makes you, you? What lays about you like smelling salts to awaken you?

What are the ways you can lead yourself back to you? Get outside. Take your tribe on a trek up the mountain. Anoint yourself in oils. Take a long bath and rub the silkiest butters into your skin. In your journal, make a list of the people, places, things that remind you of who you are, that make you feel alive. Keep it close. Refer to it when you feel yourself begin to wander.

THE BODY NEVER LIES

What is your body telling you?

Intuition, that fickle friend, is found through a physical map that we get by listening to our bodies. Our heart literally speaks through our guts. This is where the term "gut instincts" comes from. We all know that feeling of either elation (yes!) or fear (no!) and how it feels in our bellies. Before we even speak, we feel it.

So many times we are too worried about the "how." *How do I do this? How do I write? How do I paint? How do I tell the truth? How do I love?*

We are taught to ignore our feelings and to let logic rule our choices. Because of this, we are quick to dismiss what rises in the belly because it lacks tangible proof. But those first feelings, that gut instinct, is not to be ignored. Look back over the years that have made up your life and count all of the moments where you went against your instinct. What was the result? And what about all of the times when you went by feeling, even when it didn't make sense to you or anyone else?

Ask yourself questions:
> *Does this food feel good in my body?*
> *Is this friendship nourishing for my spirit?*
> *Does this work satisfy my soul?*

How does your body feel when you ask these questions? Does it open up? Close up? Does it become shaky or tired, bright or vibrant? These feelings are the voice of your intuition.

As you move on to other questions the feelings will continue to arise and you'll recognize them no matter the question or scenario. The more you practice tuning into this voice, the more your confidence will grow. The voice helps you make better choices because you already know who you are and what you want. This is how you learn the language of your own intuition.

The body is a map. Anything that's coming up, you can find it in the body. Many stresses manifest as illness, and joy can manifest as glowing skin and supreme health. The two are always intertwined.

Intuition is a gift we are given in this lifetime. If we pay attention and learn to use it, our lives can be completely transformed. A lot of people shy away from learning about it because it seems ethereal and hard to pin down. That's why we start with the body. Intuition speaks through the body, and once you tune in, it won't be so hard to figure out. There are other cues as well: mood changes are an indicator of intuition.

When I go against my truth, I start to get irritable and grumpy. When I align with my truth, I feel peaceful and relieved.

Listening to your intuition

Find a quiet place and a time where you can sit for 20 minutes without interruption. Bring your journal. Close your eyes and take 3 deep breaths.

First ask yourself: Who am I?

Set a timer for 10 minutes and list all the things you know that you are in that moment. It doesn't have to make sense; you can be love, cold, soft cotton, a rabbit. Just write the words that dance into your mind. When the timer is done read over your list.

Next, ask yourself: What do I know?

Set the timer for another 10 minutes and list all of the things you know. You might know the color of your godson's hair, the speed of the wind, you're ready to end a relationship or start a new one.

Trust your knowing. Listen to your gut. Learn the language of your own intuition and decipher the language of your inner voice.

REWRITING THE STORY OF PERFECTION

My relationship to my body is complicated. I remember thinking about dieting as a young girl. For so many of us there is very little love with the body, starting at a young age. I want to take a stand right now with each of you to shift that. We need to love ourselves deeply, and that includes loving our bodies just as they are. Of course we want to be healthy and feel amazing, but what I have found is that truly loving my body as it is inspires me to live **in** my body. What does living in my body mean?

- It means appreciating the imperfections
- It means not numbing out through food and negative thinking
- It means resting when I need to, and eating when I am hungry

So how do I do this, you might ask?

Well, it's not always easy, but I feel that it is very much a priority. I work on it daily. I talk kindly to my body. I offer gratitude for all that this beautiful body has given to me. I listen to her: for instance, if I have a headache, maybe what I'm eating isn't good for me. Or maybe I need more water. Or more sleep. Even if I don't solve the problem right away or act to change it, the awareness is an important step for me. If I am aching, I ask, "What do I need to hear from you, body?"

And then I listen …

- What would it take to love your body today?
- What would you have to let go of?

My guess is you will have to let go of some pretty strong ideas and beliefs around how you "should" look. As women, this is one of our toughest calls to action. To let go of what we believe beauty is, and instead, let beauty BE.

There is a story I would like to share with you:

One of my dearest friends passed away from cancer two years ago. I had known her since I was 16 years old. She was older than me and she was a bright light in my life. She was so incredibly generous. I remember so many beautiful things about her and I also remember how critical she was of her body. During her last months, her body was so thin, and her cheekbones were showing deeply and I remember looking at photos of her and thinking that this look—this face—this is the face that so many equate with being thin and being beautiful. My dear friend was finally "thin" but she was dying.

This is a dramatic thing to say but I was struck at how insane we can be about the body.

True beauty comes from radiance and grace and heart centered living. Someone who we might view as the most beautiful woman with the perfect body … none of that matters if she isn't healthy. Only heart, mind and soul will radiate true beauty. My dear friend is no longer here to talk to me or to hold her granddaughter's hand, but I truly believe we can learn from her journey. That to me is the greatest gift.

Being kind to yourself is a practice that requires great discipline and breaking old habits. Changing the story you are telling about yourself takes discipline and dedication. Again, there is strength in the softness. Accepting yourself may seem weak, but it is the strongest thing you can do.

Come back to your body. She's waiting for you.

Wholeness, forgiveness

In Japan they have a practice called *kintsugi*, golden joinery, or the act of repairing broken pottery with gold. The idea is that instead of dismissing a well-loved object as no longer loveable or useable, you simply fill the cracks with gold. In this way the item remains whole.

Many of us are working toward this feeling of wholeness, often confusing wholeness with perfection. Can you allow yourself to embrace your imperfections? Can you pour gold in your cracks? Could you then hold your life, hold yourself? Move toward acceptance...move toward love. In order to do that, first forgive yourself for all those times you chose the bad relationship, misplaced your anger, didn't speak up. Forgive yourself for all the times you hesitated or went against your truth.

This week in your journal, write a letter to yourself, like a mother to a child, and forgive yourself for the things you did and didn't do, for what you knew or didn't know.

> Dear Me,
> I forgive you.
> I forgive you for...
> ....
> And I still love you. You are my gold.

SELF LOVE AND CARE

How can you live a life with love and joy?

When the voice within us berates and judges, our bodies actually beg for nourishment and warmth. Yet so many of us don't know how to give that to ourselves. We easily make meals for others rarely thinking of what we want to eat. Perhaps we make meals for others and then eat only leftovers, or only a snack. We must take care of ourselves. It is truly the only way that we can take care of others.

What we crave is what we need.

Sometimes what we crave seems impossible in a busy life: rest, relaxation, quiet. Or friendship, laughter tea, travel, adventure, knowledge. Whatever it is, listen to it. Write these needs down as you go throughout your days. These are notes from the universe, reminders. Can we take simple steps toward self-love and kindness? Can the inner dialogue become deeply nourishing? Can we protect ourselves without being too rigid? Sometimes maybe it's better to just eat the ice cream than to stress out about not eating it. Every day is different.

Self-love starts within. It means looking in the mirror and not judging or it means not looking in the mirror or not weighing yourself. It means not comparing. It means giving love and allowing yourself to receive love. It means when someone compliments you, say "thank you" rather than brushing it off. It means you sleep when you are tired. It means your body is important, not just for providing food or shelter or children, but for being the vehicle **that you are using to live this life — the temple that embodies your spirit; the vessel that makes your love human.**

Perhaps we know when to make ourselves a pot of tea, when it's time to gather in a sacred circle, when we need healing touch through massage. But how often do we bow to the altar of self and express love and gratitude for the way your body moves? How often do we practice self-forgiveness, grant ourselves grace, praise the way we've managed to navigate this life and live another day?

There is self-care and there is self-love. Many of us are great at the former, but we often mistake our acts of self-care for acts of self-love. Some of us need to work on both. We practice self-care through the gifts we give ourselves that show that we care for and appreciate our well-being. Self-love is that full-bodied belief that we are worthy of the care and love we need and deserve, without condition. This means that you are kind to yourself even if you have not reached the elusive finish line. Self-love is when we celebrate our bodies, when we give ourselves permission to be present in our skin, when we embrace our inner light. Self-love is when we dance with abandon and sing from the back of the throat.

When we want to love ourselves more, we start by loving our bodies more. Can you buy yourself a massage this month? If you can't, start saving $20 a month until you can. Make a special jar for it. So many women I know feel that a massage is a frivolous expense, when really it does more for us than many other medicines because it includes touch, rest, relaxation and healing intention. Think luxury and love.

What do these words conjure for you? You are a woman. The divine feminine resides in you, you are embodied grace. Your body is a gift for you and for anyone who loves you. Say thank you to her, that beautiful body of yours. Breathe into softness and acceptance. You will still be loved, even if you accept yourself just as you are. Be the Empress, the Queen. Allow yourself this grace and power.

A soft, quiet love
can change the world.

Self-love Inventory

When we're deep in self-love, we radiate. Our hearts shine through our eyes, we're fierce, graceful, compassionate, tender, vulnerable, and strong. We are immovable and unstoppable. How do we get there?

Consider these things:

What do I love about myself when I look in the mirror? (Be honest. No one reads this but you). Can I forgive myself when I stumble in challenging conversations? Do I ask for help when I need it? Do I love myself when I am down and out as much as I love myself when I'm vibrant and healthy?

Make a list of all the things you love about yourself. Don't stop until you've written 3o. Yes, 3o. If you come up with more, even better. Work on this list throughout the week. No need to rush yourself. (Let this list be a slow work of art.) Get to know yourself as you move through it. Chances are that for some, this will take work. Sometimes we have to pick through the negative self-talk to find those loving words. And if you're still stuck, think back to the loving words of others. What have your kindreds said to you, about you, that made you feel warm?

If you love your smile, choose to smile more. If you love your ankle, adorn it. Pick one of those things and choose to live it out each day. Consider coming back to this exercise now and again.

Self-love is an unending project, and we need all the help we can get.

The Language of Intuition

Uncover and understand the language of intuition through your body:

Tell a story about a time you listened to your intuition, even when someone doubted you or pressured you not to. Recall the experience. How did it feel beforehand and afterwards? Did you feel it in your gut or somewhere else? What did you know? Who resisted you, if anyone? Was there a certain thing or moment that made you listen to yourself?

 ...

Now, recall a story about when you heard your intuition, but you went against it for some reason. What did that feel like? Why did you doubt yourself? Were there external influences? Tell the story here. Again, remember to write down the physical feelings you remember.

✎ ...

When you think back to these stories, what are the feelings and emotions that you associate with your inner voice telling you the truth? Write down what you can remember. The feelings can be physical or psychic, but tune into these memories and pull everything out. Intuitive language shows up in the body. Where does yours speak first?

 ...

What are the main parts of your body that you associate with
your intuition? Which parts of your body react first to intuitive
communication?

✎ ...

Who are your allies? We all have allies when it comes to intuition. These are people who help us trust ourselves. Children and loved ones can often be allies, or affirming reflectors. Our allies can plants, rituals or places. There are also people who discourage us from listening to our intuition and encourage fear. Write about both of these here:

✎ ...

How does your body feel around your allies? How does it feel when you are receiving an affirming reflection of your truth? On the flipside, what does it feel like when you are around people or places that interfere with your intuition?

✎ ...

Whew! This is a lot of deep stuff. Hopefully by now you are starting to see how much inner power you hold and how much wisdom you already contain without changing anything.

Through your writing you will start to see some patterns in how your inner voice emerges through your body into your life. Noticing these patterns is how we start to hone our tools. To go further with your intuition, a key exercise is to NOTICE and then PAUSE.

Over the next week(s), start to pause when you feel those feelings and when your intuitive hotspots become activated. Use this page to jot notes about when/where/why/how this is coming up. Revisit this page any time you wish.

Journal

Journal

BEAUTY
EMERGE

BEAUTY EMERGE

Your heart,
your beautiful heart.
Keeping your heart open even when the world is aching
is a radical act.
We do it because it is The Work.
It is the portal into the world we desire.

It starts with gratitude::
Feeling grateful,
Being grateful..
Living in gratitude.

Building my life on gratitude.
Building the house that I live in, painting the
walls, finishing the roof with gratitude.
Thank you for this door.
Thank you for this home.
Thank you for this opportunity, and this one and
this one.
Thank you for the challenge that breaks me wide open.
Thank you for the food and the hands that prepared
the food.
Thank you for these hands and this breath and this
one and this one too...
Thank you, thank you, thank you.

When I was younger and only had myself to think
about, my dear friend and mentor Kathleen would
suggest I do things that put me in service whenever
I was struggling with an issue. I understand now
what she was teaching me.
How can I serve?
How can I live in service?

Being of service and living in gratitude are the
gateways to my peace of mind, and my peace of mind
is my wealth.
Holding my heart with reverence and care are
exquisite acts of self care.

My beauty is not for sale.
My heart is a vessel of love.
My beauty is radiant and lives within me.
my heart is supporting me and holding me up.
My beauty is effervescent and a reflection of my soul.
My heart is strong and steady.

Beauty Emerge....

INTIMACY WITH OURSELVES

When we open the heart, we radiate love. This month, bring love to all that you do. Use your foundation. Let it be simple. Don't worry too much about if you are doing it "right" or if you are where you "should be." Let it be how it is, and let yourself be who you are. I promise you, you're doing a good job.

When I talk about the heart and the heart center, I am talking about the energy around our hearts: it is this energy that rules our truth and the way we love and feel. It is an actual vibration that we put out. The heart-center is a physical space as well as an energetic and metaphorical space for love and compassion.

When the heart center is open, we feel differently. We aren't defensive. We don't feel scarcity. It's easier to see the interconnectedness of all beings, and therefore compassion and understanding are easier to experience. Opening the heart removes us from limited self-centered thinking such as "What about me?" or "Will I have enough?"

The heart center (or heart chakra) is also about boundaries and immunity. Having good boundaries ensures that our heart centers are safe from unwanted energies. This type of protection is important so that we let in only what we determine to be good for us. Negative stuff is always around, but it doesn't need to be allowed in. Openness is good but only with boundaries and awareness. If you are feeling overwhelmed by other people's emotions or energies, it's time to start having better boundaries around your heart center.

However, if you are feeling emotionally dependent or like your sense of self is diluted or attached to other people, it's time to step into your heart center a bit more and really open that up so it can be active and strong.

You probably have heard the phrase, "from the heart." When someone speaks or creates from the heart, it is what speaks to the world loudest. This is what's possible with a balanced heart center. Speaking from the heart gives each person a feeling of being truly present with the other. **This is the basis of real intimacy.** The first 3 chakras (from root to navel) are ruled by a sense of ME. As we step into the heart, we go beyond ME to WE. This is the 4th chakra: heart communication. "Heart-to-heart" communication does not mean that you are always sweet or agreeable. It only means that you are compassionate and truthful. Yogi Bhajan says "truth spoken with fear is a lie." Speaking with truth and kindness together is the true power and gift of the heart-center.

Blocks in the diaphragm affect the heart. All breathing meditations stimulate the heart center and help remove blocks.

Beauty Emerge is about intimacy with our lives and with who we are. Living within our lives starts by sharing our authentic selves with others. Sharing our true selves is scary and it takes courage. It takes knowing when to say no and when to say yes. Stop watching from the sidelines, afraid to share your gifts or yourself with the world. It's time to share who you are.

Become aware of your heart center. Stretch it daily. Open it up to the sun, the sky, your loved ones. As you adjust your body and your surroundings, you also adjust your inner self and begin to expand outward into the space you have created.

If you can see this moment as an opportunity to bring presence and grace to your life, then even the chaos and the hard bits hold beauty.

Mind & Body Care

This week's prompt is an extensive list of Yogic practices for your mind and body. Choose whichever ones feel good to you and practice them this entire month, or as you feel called.

Remember, this is not medical advice. Use your good judgement and consult a medical practitioner when needed and trust your intuition regarding these suggestions.

Beloved Rest ~

These are some yogic sleep tips that Yogi Bhajan shared with women at his yearly women's camp. I have found them very valuable.

Before bed, rinse your feet in cold water and dry them briskly. Take some oil (almond/olive/whatever you have) and rub a bit into the crown of your head, the outer ear and, inside each nostril. Before you lie down, meditate to clear the mind. Then lie on your back and gently and consciously relax every part of your body. Sleeping on the right side will shift your breathing to the left nostril and bring deep and relaxed sleep.

Beloved Belly ~

Some yogic eating tips:

> Light breakfast
> Substantial, healthy lunch
> Energy boosting drink in afternoon
> Light dinner

For eating schedules, tune into what your body really needs. Each of us align to a slightly different routine and schedule. Do you have a special recipe for an afternoon smoothie/energy drink?

Yogi Bhajan suggested for women over age 28 to supplement their diet with high-quality, cold-pressed oils first thing in the morning: 2 tablespoons of almond, sesame, olive (combined or alone) along with 1 tablespoon of ground flax seed every day. This helps to lower cholesterol, reduce fat in the body, keep skin healthy, reduce hunger, cleanse body of toxins, and it is also an excellent source of protein.

For added benefit, I like to add 2-3 tablespoons of water-soluble liquid chlorophyll in a glass of water daily.

Here is a recipe for my favorite yogic dish. (This recipe is cleansing and is great for skin. I ate this a lot when shooting *The Matrix*.

YOGI MYSH

> 4 celery stalks
> 4-5 medium zucchinis
> 1 bunch parsley
> 1 sprig mint
> 1/2 teaspoon black pepper

> Steam all together until soft (layer the celery on bottom, then zucchini, then parsley and mint). Next, blend together; I like to add the water that they steamed in. Then add pepper.
> Serve with some cottage cheese on top (or Parmesan, or nothing!) I squirt Bragg's Liquid Aminos on top. Enjoy.

Beloved Body ~

Here are some yogic skin care ideas to do when you want to feel extra beautiful and loved.

01   Gather some oat flour, rose water and almond oil and combine them to make a paste. Use this as a gentle exfoliator for your skin. Rinse, and then smooth a layer of raw honey directly onto your face and allow to rest for a few minutes. Rinse the honey with warm water and then rinse again with cooled chamomile tea. Pat dry. Enjoy the cleanliness!

02   Massage (organic, plain) yogurt into your chest and face like a mask. Then take a warm bath, allowing the mask to dry on your face while the water becomes a creamy milky color from the yogurt on your body. Soak for a half hour in this divine milk bath. Next, rinse your face with warm water followed by a rinse of either water and apple cider vinegar or water and lemon juice. (3 to 4 tablespoons of juice or vinegar to one quart of water). Let the vinegar or lemon rinse stay on the skin to tone. Do not dry off with a towel: let yourself dry naturally so that your skin can absorb the rinse. This is especially nourishing after your moon cycle is completed.

For exercise, WALK. Get a sweat going every day.

Beloved Moon ~

Eat sautéed almonds with honey on the first three days of your cycle:
Sauté almonds in almond or sesame oil. Add honey to taste. Eat this in
the morning.

While you are menstruating, refrain from breath of fire and make sure
to modify your yoga practice so that it is gentle.
Take an 11 minute nap daily.

NOTE: If you are peri or post-menopausal, many of these
recommendations are perfect for you as well, as they help to balance
and soothe the systems. Doing Kundalini yoga daily and making
sure to exercise is great for shifting hormones, and meditating and
breathwork help to steady your sleep patterns and reduce stress.

RELEASING PRESSURE + LETTING THE LIGHT IN

There is power in action.

We don't need to simmer in the anticipation or fear of change or sharing. When we feel pressured about something, the release-valve lies in taking action to catalyze a shift. Then we move out of the pressure zone. If we stay under pressure, it creates stress and then it is harder to be graceful. It's easy to trap ourselves in a state of pressure! Remember, when the pressure is on, get started, and the pressure comes off. Start with small steps. Make a list and start with the first tiny thing.

The first thing to do is to notice when the pressure is on. Pressure can sometimes be invisible, and instead it manifests in us being short-tempered, or sad, or preoccupied. Sometimes we don't want to look at the pressure—the thing that needs to be done or decid. It's a process of clearing away cobwebs, or cleaning windows. Have you ever been driving and you don't notice how dirty the windshield is, but once you clean it—you can't believe the difference? Apply this to your life. Where is there tension, fear or pressure? Where is it resting quietly? It's time to scrub it out so that you can see clearly and so the sun can shine in.

Just as you clean the windows of your home and your car, remember to clean the windows of your body and spirit. But how to do this?

Well, sometimes when I want to work on the inside, I start with the outside.

Perhaps it is time to literally clean your windows. Have they been cleaned recently? Which are the ones you look out of the most? Start there. Look into the corners of your home: are they dusty? Look at the places you use the most—are they messy and stagnant? Clean them up. By honoring our spaces in these ways, we honor ourselves. This is a good month to take your altar pieces out into the sun and bathe them in light and water. Perhaps this is a good month to do this to yourself too.

By actively starting on the "outside," we remove blockages on the inside, too. Things come up and dissipate; we realize what we need, and where our actions need to go next.

Lists

This week, let's make some lists. Get out your journal and sit somewhere peaceful or beautiful, somewhere you love to be.

With each of the questions below, write down the first thing that comes to you. Try not to think about it, if you can. Be loose. Even if your answer seems surprising or irrational, write it down.

> What needs attention?
> What is bothering you?
> What do you want to do?
> Where do you want to go?

Revisit these questions any time. You can have multiple answers to each one. What do you see in your answers? Is there something in your space or in your daily life that needs attention? Choose one of your answers and expand on it in your journal. What will you do to explore it further?

COMPASSION + STEPPING INTO LOVE

Every time you judge someone, can you see how you are similar to them? This is the secret of compassion, and it lies at the heart of the Golden Rule, which is at the core of all love and peace.

Compassion and courage are both heart-centered. I believe it takes courage to have compassion. It's easy to hide behind judgement and blame, but when we take a moment to see if we can reach for compassion instead, everything changes. Not just for us, but for the people around us as well. Retraining our reactions is some of the hardest work we will ever do. Reactions are our autopilot: they are instant and preprogrammed. This is why they are so hard to shift, yet when we begin to shift them, it feels incredible, like a deep cleansing.

I look for elegance and grace in everything It's up to me to find these things and to embody them. When we act in compassion, we begin to change ourselves and the world around us because acting in compassion is acting in love. When we act in love, we attract love. What you give, you receive. In a situation where you feel confused or frustrated, take a moment to consider: what is the most generous thing I can do right now? What can I give? Who needs the most love in this situation?

When I am overwhelmed, tired or spread thin, my inclination is to withdraw, or to hold tightly to the resources I have. Sometimes I become snappy or impatient. What I've learned is if I can gracefully step into love in these moments, then I immediately receive love back (which is just what I need in those moments). When we gather our strength and step into love, love steps into us.

If someone around you is snappy or rude, impatient or spread thin—what do they need? Love comes in many forms. It's been said by hundreds of wise teachers that we must never underestimate the power of a small gesture: a kind act, a small hug, a compliment. In your home, imagine if someone told you that tonight they are going to do the dishes so that you can take a bath. Heaven! The simple things! So powerful!

Gratitude List

I have been very inspired by my amazing teacher Paramatma Siri Sadhana who has me write down lots of gratitudes as a practice - 111 to be exact!

I want you to do that this week. Think how great it will feel to see so many pages of gratitude for your beautiful life. I recommend doing this in one sitting. Get some tea and maybe some snacks. Sit somewhere beautiful, where the sunlight or fresh air can be on your face.

It's amazing what happens when you write this many. You begin to see the seemingly small things as incredible. The last time I did this, here are some things I wrote down:

91. I am grateful for tea

92. I am grateful for softness

93. I am grateful for truth

94. I am grateful for colored pencils

95. I am grateful for surrender

96. I am grateful for grace

97. I am grateful for this experience

EMERGENCE

It's time to remember your dreams and our passions. Let them emerge! Clear away the ties that bind them, and open the curtains to let in the light.

My teacher Paramatma says to look to what breaks your heart and breaks it open, that your calling lies there. Often we try to hide from our darkness, or try to hide it from people we love. It's vulnerable to look there, or share it. This is what true vulnerability is: to welcome the weakness in as part of you. The fear of rejection rises up strong in these moments. I urge you to push through—lean on your meditation and/or prayer. As you learn to love yourself, love will pour in from other places.

This "darkness" is not always obvious. It's not as ominous as it seems. It's just where we are hung up on ourselves. Where is your shame? When we think about these stories, we feel uncomfortable, that it is exactly where we need to start. But how?

In this modern world of spiritual seekers, we often hear about welcoming the pain and looking at the darkness. But how do we really do that? What does it really feel like to welcome the darkness so that the light can be pure? I am still figuring this out. But here's what I've learned: Surrendering feels awkward. It feels uncomfortable, literally and physically. It makes me want to leave somewhere, or cry, or it just feels frustrating. These feelings are the teachers. The "shadow work" is often just looking at where we are ashamed, and then addressing it. It is sitting in those awkward feelings. Why the shame? How can we let it go? An act of love.

Have you asked your lover or your child lately what they are ashamed of? With a simple act of love, you can help them let it go. Because their shame carries no weight for you. You might bring laughter to it for them, release the pressure of the burden, the secrecy, the guilt. Sometimes, it really is that simple. Because I've seen this, I know it is possible for each of us.

Let's make our own shame weightless. To do this we must look at it, give it a name, give it wings, let it fly away. This is what it means to forgive yourself.

Unhook it from yourself. Take the tiny hooks out and let it go. It's okay. No really—it is. You are loved.

Tenderness

Is there a story you keep deep down inside because it seems like too much? Can you forgive yourself for it? Can you give it wings?

I had a friend who used to say she would never date a man who hadn't had his heart broken. She insisted that the men she date be whole from the process of overcoming loss, rejection, sadness and grief. "Heartbreak makes you whole," she said. We can apply this to ourselves. Our imperfections are what make us whole. They are what shape us and teach us to love and to be loved.

Getting awkwardly cozy with our shame and our mistakes sets us free. A good way to do this is by writing down the stories and myths you tell yourself. Another good way to do this is by sharing these stories with a compassionate friend or listener. One who won't judge you or reinforce shame. As we pull these stories out of our depths, we drag them out from under rocks where they have been stuck, and allow them to finally breathe, dissolving in the light.

Pick a story from your mossy, depths and write it down. It might feel uncomfortable. If you don't want to write it, say it aloud to yourself, tell it to your angels. Imagine the story on the wings of a butterfly, and let it fly. Picture it being exposed to air and sunshine and then turning to dust.

By clearing away the dust, our true beauty emerges.

Sat nam.

Releasing pressure and clearing corners

This month you are **CLEARING IT OUT** so that your BEAUTY can EMERGE. It's not always about building. Sometimes it's about clearing things away so your true essence can rise up and shine. What could use some cleaning in your life right now? Write down the first few things that come to mind (car, kitchen, bedroom, etc.)

✎ …

Of all of these places or things, which is the one you want to do the LEAST? Why?

✎ …

Look at your "least" favorite choice. This is where you start because this is where you're blocked. We start there where things feel stuck, no matter how hard it is. The reward will feel even bigger.

Write down some ways to make this fun. Invite a girlfriend to come help you; turn on a playlist; make yourself a delicious tonic; throw open the windows and sing while you do it.

✎ ...

Some extra suggestions:

- Get out the garbage bags in case you want to purge some things and free up space and energy
- Organize a clothing swap with friends to get rid of items that don't fit anymore
- Rearrange your furniture
- Look to forgotten corners for creative places to start
- Need to free up some creative energy? Clean up your workspace
- Need to feel more rested? Clean up the bedroom.
- Be mindful of electronics and how they are permeating sacred spaces. Be especially mindful of their presence in bedrooms. Be creative with ways to incorporate electronics in your home without them feeling invasive. Consider organizing cords in baskets and putting a scarf over your TV.

As you begin some of these cleaning projects, you will feel some energy shift, and things will become more clear. Is anything coming up for you? Are you realizing other things were stuck that you were ignoring? Write them down here so that you can remember to work on those things, too.

Finally, this is a great time to revitalize your altar. Altars are living things, and they move and shift, like anything else. Clean your treasures, add fresh flowers, do whatever you feel called to do.

✎ ...

Journal

Journal

ALCHEMY
SPEAKS

ALCHEMY SPEAKS

I am speaking my life into being.
I am speaking me into being.

That story I love to tell, the one about how
disappointed I was. That story I tell so that I can
relate and connect and bond.
That story that sends me into panic that is living
only inside my mind...

I don't want or need to tell old stories that are
habitual.
I will speak my beautiful, glorious life into action
by speaking it out loud.
By breathing it into being,
By imagining it
as so.

Yes, I have been through so much and I will not
pretend that I haven't.
I won't lie and say I'm rosy when I am having a hard
time,
BUT...

I will be more inclined to rewrite the story … to
catch myself when I start to compare complain and
gossip.
I will see that wanting to tell that story again may
be a sign that I'm lonely and I need to find other
ways to connect.
I don't need to bond over hardships.
I can bond over hope and dreams and lifting up.
I will empower you to step into your greatness, your
beauty,
and I will do the same for me.

The old habitual stories that no longer serve must
be let go through discipline and devotion.

If we want our lives to be a true reflection of our
souls,
Then we need to STOP playing small by repeating the
stories that don't serve us.

Share yourself with the world but pay attention to
the way you are speaking about yourself...
Be a good friend to yourself and treat yourself with
respect
through words and actions.

Speak your life into being.

HOW DO I COMMUNICATE WITH THE WORLD?

We create our reality with the words we speak. It's time to break our bad habits of negative, dis-empowering language. This includes negative self-talk and negative gossip.

This takes discipline. Don't I know it!

We bring the bad habits to the fire and let them go in order to create a new story. Ask yourself, *What is my authentic voice? What do I want to say: What do I want people to hear?*

Communicating with the world is a large part of our lives. Though we each have our own inner world, daily interactions are what fill up our days. We all know how a sequence of small, pleasant interactions can make us feel elated, right? Similarly, one tiny negative interaction can ruin our whole day. Being mindful of our own communication is one way that we can work toward creating smooth and pleasant days. As we do this, we also give this gift to other people.

When we go through the day complaining, ranting, or criticizing, we get back the energy we put out. Maybe we are complaining in hopes of receiving compassion and empathy but there's a better way to get what we need. Go about your day complimenting, being generous, and lifting up others. See what happens.

How do you speak to people? To loved ones? To strangers? What assumptions do you make? An unkind word is often sharper than a knife. Be aware of the communication tools you have and how you use them.

Centered in the throat chakra, communication is connected to our health, clarity and confidence. When the chakra is open and strong, we feel clearer and brighter.

When the chakra is weak it results in shyness, cloudy communication, insecurity, and even throat or voice problems. Much of this manifests as a fear of other people's opinions and judgements, rather than resilience. I need to stay rooted in our own confidence and choices.

Be mindful of complaining and gossip. These words do no good for you or the world around you.

I speak kindly and clearly and truthfully. I am impeccable with my word.

Blue & Turquoise

The color associated with the throat chakra is blue. Think of clear blue waters and how they represent clarity, purity, power and beauty. This week, get creative with blue. Do you have a necklace with blue stones or beads? Give it a loving wash and then wear it with reverence to honor your voice to enhance your clarity. Do you have a blue dress or shirt? Wear it with the intention of speaking clearly and kindly to all who cross your path.

HOW DO I COMMUNICATE TO MYSELF?

Thought our words, we create our world through our words.

What kind of house do you want to live in? How do you want to treat yourself? Negative self talk can be either obvious or subtle. Either way, your body hears it and assimilates it. Do things feel hopeless? Fight it with words. Say "My life is full of possibility!" Do you feel uncomfortable with your body? Fight it with words. Say "I love my body and that it allows me to connect with people I love."

Speech is powerful. It is powerful in politics, religion, at home, in our bedrooms. Its power is never decreased unless it is silenced.

I encourage you to focus on using this power to feed your soul. Speak kindly to yourself. Truly. When you are feeling stressed out, step back. What is the source? Can the kindness start there? Say to yourself, "Dang, woman, you are handling this really well, all things considered. You deserve a bath." Or whatever it may be. Imagine if your situation was a friend's. Wwhat would you say to her? Say it to yourself.

PROMPT

Every thought,
every word we speak
creates our reality.

Memorize a Poem

Spend some time searching for a poem that instills a sense of beauty within you. Memorize it, learn it by heart. Say it out loud. Again.

Write it here so you can refer back to it at a later point.

HOW DO I COMMUNICATE MY NEEDS?

Life is all consuming and it's easy to forget our needs altogether. In a day full of bits and pieces and driving and dishes, our needs easily fall between the cracks. This builds until it overwhelms us, and then we break down. It is our job to first be aware of our needs. This takes commitment and some moments of silence. Second, we must communicate these needs, otherwise they will not be met — by us, by partners, by children or by co-workers.

Do you need to be alone from 3-4 pm? Tell your family that's your hour. Do you need a big birthday party? Tell those who are closest to you so that it is more likely to happen. Do you need to go to bed earlier? Begin to shift things so that this is possible.

Ask yourself, *What do I need?* Once we know what we need, then we can speak it. When we don't know what we need or how to communicate it, how can we expect the other person to know our needs?

Don't expect others to read your mind. This always ends in disappointment. Be crystal clear — communicate exactly. "Could you please rub my shoulders?" "Can you make me a tea please?" Saying, "You never do anything for me" will not inspire anyone to help you. So don't let it get to that point. Even saying, "I need your support" is not clear enough. Say what kind of support you need. Sometimes we just need to be held, sometimes we need help making decisions, sometimes we need people to come help us pack boxes and move into a new house. Sometimes we are sick and need someone to come over and help with our children, or with dinner. Be as specific as you can, and everyone benefits.

Asking

Often we don't ask for what we want because we don't quite know what exactly we want. Clarity is a continued process of thought and action, not necessarily just one statement. When we are asked for something, it's wise to pause for a moment and make sure we are asking for what we truly need. Sometimes we ask for things based on an emotion, rather than need, and then we don't end up getting what we want.

This week, write down some needs in your journal. Spend some time looking at them. The day after you write them down, revisit them. Write a little more about them … where are they coming from? Can you expand on them? Who do you need to ask for help?

On the third day, look at them again. Do they still feel valid? Are you ready to ask for help? Write down exactly what and who you will ask. By now, these needs should be very clear. Re-visiting them over the course of three days as well as in writing will give you much more clarity than just thinking about them.

HOW DO I COMMUNICATE & CREATE

Asking for what we need is one of the most powerful human communication functions that we have. When we use it gracefully and clearly, we receive more than we thought possible.

This power is what initiates the manifestation of a physical reality or action by simply uttering words are planting the seed of that future manifestation.

What I speak, I become. My words are my home.

One of our greatest powers as humans is to initiate a direction or action. Many women hold a fear of being blunt. It is time to let that go. Do not let a perceived obligation to politeness hold you back from creating the life you want. Say No. Say Yes. Say what you mean. This is the power of projection.

Plant the seed.
Speak it into being.

Sing It Aloud

This week, we sing. Sing for yourself, for the dreams you hold dear. For the pain you have experienced, for the moments you won, and the moments you lost. Sing for the earth and for all that she gives us. Sing a song from your childhood that you loved to sing. Look it up online and sing it again. Or find a song you love to sing in the car, in the shower, to your children. Sing it.

Singing clears out the throat chakra and removes obstacles of communication. Singing clears the pathways. Singing brings the light. Singing is a small way to grow big.

A way through every block

Things I love to do that make me feel creative:

✎ ...

Things I love to do that make me feel accomplished:

✎ ...

Things I love to do that make me feel relaxed:

✎ ...

Things I love to do that make me feel connected:

✎ ...

Take your time and fill out these lists. You don't need to do it all in one sitting. Write them over the course of a few days. Then, use this list when you are feeling stuck. Any of the things on this list can help you move in the right direction. Even if you are feeling stuck about something big like mortgages or job changes, these small actions will help you move through it, even if they seem totally unrelated.

 ...

Remember to take a peek at these lists anytime you need a reminder about how to move through, forward, and onward.

Journal

Journal

IN HER LIGHT

IN HER LIGHT

Dear intuition, the part of me that knows,
I bow to you.
I am sorry that I haven't always trusted you.
I am sorry that so many of my sisters have been
stripped of their connection to you.
I stand here today to welcome you,
to witness you, and to receive your wisdom.
My intuition is blessed.
My intuition is the sound of my highest.
My intuition lives within me and surrounds me with
protection and projection of soul.

Subtle and sometimes striking—
I hear you,
I know you,
I honor you,
I appreciate you.

Grounded am I
So that I can hear you.

Steady am I
so that I can feel you.

Open am I
so that bravely I can live in you

In my light I live
In my light I love
In my light I share
In my light I am enough.

Who do you tell your secrets to? Who knows what you love, or what you need? Who reminds you of who you truly are, when things feel lost or forgotten?

EASE AND RELAXATION

When we are relaxed, intuition flows. When we are scattered and lacking harmony with the outerworld, the disconnection makes us frenetic. It's a sign we need to slow down and recalibrate.

Creating rhythm to cultivate ease and relaxation in your full, busy life will naturally make you more intuitive and help you connect to your higher self. Creating rhythm takes effort at first, but over time is becomes easier and you can relax into it. Tune into what your body really wants, and base your rhythm off of that. Create rituals that foster rhythm.

Rituals can be easy and simple. Turn toward the subtle, the quiet, and the mundane. It's likely that there's already already ritual in your life; tea in the morning or the way you get dressed, the face wash, then the serum, then the moisturizer, in that order, every time. Perhaps the way your child wakes you up, or the way you text your honey before bed every night. Look at these small rhythms. These are your rituals. Which ones fill you up the most? Which ones feel tiring?

Appreciating these small wonders brings honor to our lives. As we create nurturing rituals, our rituals begin to support us with ease and grace. Without even thinking, we flow through our rhythms like the sun moves through the sky. And what about relaxation? Our days roll by in countless numbers and suddenly we might think, *When was the last time I relaxed*? Vacations may be so packed with activities and visitors that sometimes time slips by without enough relaxation. Then we are home again, feeling the need to recover. This amuses me. Sometimes I need a vacation to recover from my vacation!

In Fierce Grace we are working to build lives we don't need a vacation from. We are creating the spaces in our daily life, in our waking hours of normalcy. How do we relax? Do we relax on our phones, or should we turn them off? Sometimes the greatest act of rebellion is going into our bedrooms and laying down in the middle of the afternoon, don't you think?

Let's rebel by relaxing:

- Make the frozen pizza or the box of mac and cheese.
- Take the 10 minute nap.
- Say no to the party invitation.
- Say yes to sleeping in.
- Say yes to extra snuggles in your bed.
- Read the book that makes you happy, not the book that makes you smart.

However you can do it, do it.

Relax! Rejoice!

Find Your Solitude

Where do you go when you want to be alone? Go beyond relation to find your solitude. There is something sacred about silence. The world in which we live is loud. People, places, and things are constantly fighting for our attention and it takes discipline to step away, shut down, and shut off. The reward is worth it. You will emerge from your solitude with more clarity and a renewed spirit. What can you do to create a pocket of solitude in your day, or even just once a week?

Ideas:
Take a 20 minute walk in the woods.

Turn off the radio in the car.

Lay peacefully on your bed for 15 minutes.

Allow your peace to come to you in these small but holy moments.

This break from the noise, the intentional act of practicing deep listening—of hearing yourself—is one of the most nourishing acts you give yourself.

THIRD EYE

The third eye is considered the Command Chakra. It is the sixth chakra and it is also sometimes known as the "sixth sense." It is connected to your intuition and tells you which direction to go. The two eyes on your face allow you to see the normal world but the third eye gives you spiritual vision that lets you see deep within.

There are ways you can tune in more fully to your third eye. Meditation is a great tool for this, and our work in Fierce Grace connects us in this way. Connecting with your third eye or intuition is all about slowing down and breathing in, breathing out. Sometimes I like to lightly tap on my third eye to remind myself that I have this aid, this extra way of seeing. Some people like to put some light essential oils on this place to activate it.

Tuning into the third eye can be fun, it doesn't always have to be serious. I know all of you are working on your meditation practice, because you wouldn't be here with me if you weren't! That means you are all working on opening your third eye already.

A lot of this seems vague and hazy, I know. Third eye? Sixth chakra? Neither of these things can be seen or touched. The best way to connect with them is to create awareness and then stop trying! Yes. Stop trying.

When we are thinking thinking thinking about how to solve a problem, the answer seems to get farther away the more we think. Then, days later, as we run along the ocean shore or crest a viewpoint on a hike, laughing with friends, the answer settles simply into our hearts, like a feather landing on the ground. It's the path of least resistance that ultimately opens up our third eye. You are doing the work during meditation, the rest of the time it's all about softening and opening.

One of the best ways to soften and open your third eye is to smile.

As you smile, you will feel your whole face relax, and the center point, your third eye, opens up like a flower.

Making Space

Choose a corner in your home to focus on. You can choose a section of your porch or yard or simply a wall. Just focus on a physical space or area in which you'd like to experience a little more peace.

First, remove everything! Make it a blank canvas upon which you can create something new. Find new homes for the items that you no longer wish to remain in that space. Donate what you no longer need.

Now, let it breathe. Clean it. Don't rush to refill or redecorate. Give it time. Listen for the space to tell you what it wishes to become. Let your soul be the guide and see what draws you in.

Little by little, add furniture, art, flower, words of encouragement–anything that makes your heart sing–until it's no longer an area to be rushed through or avoided, but admired and adored.

Dedicate an intention to keep that place clean and clear and sacred so that it continues to be a place that gives you peace and joy.

INNOCENCE AND INTUITION (NATURAL STATE)

Intuition is freshest when we are in a place of innocence. If you look at children, they are attuned to their intuition because they haven't gone too far into the world of the ego. They speak their truth freely and they avoid unpleasant situations without guilt. "I don't like him, Mom," is not an uncommon phrase to hear from a child, no matter who is listening. We can also look to our beloved canine companions for inspiration in this matter. They, too, are masters of intuition because they simply have no ego at all and live only in love. They would never dream of pretending to be comfortable when they are not! Dogs act in pure truth because they exist in that state of natural innocence.

Often times our intuition is more accurate in the morning when we are well rested. This is also why people meditate. When I was younger I wasn't sure quite why people meditated, except I knew it helped people "chill out." Eventually I met someone who told me he meditated so that he could hear his inner voice better, and something clicked for me in that moment. When we can be in our natural state and shed the daily noise, we hear our intuition. Just like a plant that wants to grow, our intuition wants to be heard.

Getting to a place of innocence is not always easy as adults. We have many bags to carry on this proverbial train, often making it hard to frolic with wild abandon. But, it's in there! There is always the place of innocence inside of us, waiting for when we need it. Sometimes it hides out of fear or out of memory of being hurt. More often than not, we simply set innocence aside so we can get the daily things done.

Intuition and innocence are the sandy beach, the aspen grove, the walk through the forest. They are the homemade birthday cake, the afternoon sunlight falling through the window, the simplest of things and places. They are the first stretch in the morning, without thoughts of emails, phone calls, or the gas tank. They are the laundry hanging on the line, a box of overripe peaches for jam making.

Everywhere, all around you, these things surround your world. Pluck them as you would the peaches. Let them fill the space you live in, look at them. Whatever makes you feel that lightness of being, that bubble rising inside of you ... the laughter emerging, the melting of happiness ... let it all in. This is your state of innocence.

Listening to Your Truth

In our culture, we're often told what to believe. We learn a history, a language, a religion. We learn how to act and dress. Parents encourage us to follow a certain path. All of this instruction causes us to lose the innate connection to our inner voice.

What does your truth sound like?

This exericse is good for when you're in need of a little clarity or when you're having trouble discerning the voice of your own heart.

Find someplace quiet and without distraction. (I think early morning is best for this.) Before you've made contact with the outside world, open up your journal. Allow yourself to write whatever pops into your mind.

Don't filter. Don't hesitate. It is often the first thought that is the truest of true.

Ask yourself,
"What do I know to be true today?"
"Where do I feel my truth?"

OWNERSHIP

An essential part of intuition is ownership. No one owns your intuition but you. It is one of the things in life that is entirely, uniquely yours. There is no measuring stick for it, no where to crosscheck its viability or performance. Every single aspect of it comes from within. You cannot compare your inner truth to any outer truths and hope for success, because it's not there. The only measure of your intuition is in your heart. Owning your intuition does a few things: It cultivates power because you are giving your truth permission to thirve. It also cultivates strength because your truth feels heard. The reciprocal relationship you have with your intutiton will continue to strengthen exponentially as you claim it.

One of the toughest parts about intuition is doubt. Doubt comes both from within us as well as from external sources.

When you make an intuitive decision, some people will look at you funny and say, "Are you sure?" Or you might do that to ourselves! When I make a decision and sleep on it, it becomes clear to me whether or not I've made the right call. That clarity is my intuition speaking to me. If I hear doubt from someone else—a loved one especially—it throws me off balance. I question myself in a different way. It makes clarity harder to come by.

We strive for that balance and clarity. The only way for intuition to thrive is to own it. If someone questions it, look at them in the eye and you say, "Yes, I am sure. Thank you for asking!" Thank your inner voice for guidance. Allow it to be what it is, even if it tells you what other people don't want to hear, or even what you don't want to hear. That's the thing about the inner voice—it speaks the truth, and truth is not always pleasant.

Ownership feels different to everyone. It's a big deal to take ownership of your inner voice. It's a feminine and powerful thing to do.

Owning our inner-knowing is like climbing a mountain you weren't quite sure about, but felt called to ascent. Or like when you drag yourselves out of the house because we know we need some fresh air, and you walk for miles and witnessing an electric sunset. Freedom means you can spread your wings, feel your heart, and sing to the world. It also means you can carry your truth quietly in yourself, letting it lead the way.

Through a Child's Eye

Children have an inspiring way of seeing the world. It's not uncommon for leaves and rocks and flower petals to make their way into a house in which a child lives. And these things are not a mess, but a reminder of the beauty that exists within our reach. It's also a reminder to always be looking for those tiny miracles that sometimes go unnoticed.

What do you think would happen if you began to move through the world as a child again? What would you see? What would you touch? Set aside some time today to be outside. You don't even need to leave your neighborhood.

In fact, you can probably just open the front door. Let your eyes scan the sky and then look toward the ground. What do you notice?

What simple but beautiful treasures are there to behold?

Begin to collect them, just as a child would do. Set them aside somewhere special such as on your altar and let the joy of finding beauty be easy and simple.

Vibrate the Cosmos and it Will Clear the Path

What are the cosmos, exactly? The cosmos are the expansive unknown, the stars and the galaxy, the vast space surrounding us. Sometimes we get so caught up in ourselves, that simply looking up to the cosmos can remind us that there is so much more, and that brings us peace.

This week, practice laying on your back and looking at the sky. You can do it during the day or night, alone or with others, but do it daily if you can, and see how your perspective begins to change.

Here are some things to consider. Use the space on this page to write your thoughts and answers:

What vibration are you most attracted to? What words do you love to hear, or what words do you look forward to in your daily life, from friends, lovers, peers, at work, etc.? Write them all down so you can look at them. Think about ways that YOU can begin to say these words more often. See what begins to change.

✎ ...

Choosing one of the words from your list, use this page to make a collage (or drawing!) inspired by that word and that vibration.

✎ ...

After you've completed your artwork, feel free to hang it somewhere you can see it daily if you'd like, or just keep it in your Fierce Grace notebook or journal. The art will help you remember the vibration to which you are drawn. And what we want to receive, we can often get by giving.

Remember, when you need help, just look up at the stars and take a breath. You are supported.

Sat Nam. X

Journal

Journal

WONDER
WOMAN

WONDER WOMAN

Like the moon, I change.
Oh sweet and sacred moon,
you give me everything I need to hold myself through
the tides of my life.
I anchor to you in gratitude and in absolute
surrender.
It has taken me my whole life to give you the credit
you deserve, and the gratitude you never expect.
If only my younger me had known the power of you.
I sigh in relief when I align with you.
I choose you over mainstream ways of telling time
and setting intentions.
You watch over me, you guide me, you support me, and
inspire me.

What can I do for you, Beauty Moon?
How can I thank you?

I hear you clearly respond:

Be all that you are.
Be full like me.
Accept yourself.
Love yourself.
Shine brightly, and trust the times when you go
inward and need shelter.
Know that you, too, are like me... full of everything
you need to thrive.
Be steady, woman. You are held, you are seen, and
you are enough.

I wrote this song when I was 11 years old:

I was walking around the corner, and what do you
think I saw?
I saw a star as bright as the sun.
I thought it would be rather fun
to be up in the air with that little star.
To be flying up above with that little star.
The very next day that little star was gone.
My eyes were filled with tears because there's no
more fun.
To be up in the air with that little star to be flying
up above with that little star.

~~~

May we look up to the sky and feel supported by the
sky, the moon, the sun, and the stars.
May we remember our innocence in the magic of the
sky.
May we have hope where we feel fear.
May we be held by the earth.
May we have faith when we feel hardened.
May we choose to live our lives with a connection to
our souls.
May we remember who we are.
And that we are ...

Exquisite.

All love to you women.

NEW MOON: RENEWAL

I love the moon and I try to live by it as much as I can. I love measuring time in this way.

My intention is to line up with the lunar powers that be, no matter where I am or what phase the moon is in. It is my hope to share with you this information and these tools so that no matter what, you can look to the moon for guidance and support.

Learning about the rhythms and cycles of the moon teaches us to know our needs without consulting external sources. Outside sources will always have information but the moon is a constant timekeeper and consultant, regarless of technology, access or rules.

Our task is to let go of any limited thoughts we have around the moon and her meaning—hold only to what feels true to you. Many people feel the new moon is a time for new beginnings, but if you feel deep in your heart that it's a time for closure or endings, then so be it. You decide what it means to you. The moon is always in flux and so the meanings are always shifting and flowing.

ABOUT THE NEW MOON

The new moon is the point of total darkness with no moonlight in the sky. Darkness is an opportunity for rebirth, regrowth, and for shedding. The vessel is empty so it can be filled again. The dirt is rich and tilled so seeds can be planted. Perhaps you are not called to ritual or celebration, but still this new moon speaks to you and helps you shed, release, renew, rebuild.

In Lisa Lister's book *Love Your Lady Landscape*, she writes that the new moon is when "the moon is directly between the Earth and the Sun, and therefore hidden. This is a great time for planning new beginnings and new undertakings, while having a little 'cave time' to read, watch movies, and pamper your sweet self."

Every new moon brings with it a particular feeling. It is up to you to find out what these feelings are. I invite you to abandon any preconceived notion you've ever had about the new moon and tune in to **you**. By tracking moon cycles and using a moon journal, you can discover patterns you never knew about before, and you'll be able to depend on the moon for guidance, allowance, gentleness, and strength.

For me, I have found so much relief in the moon. It's taught me that sometimes I will be strong, sometimes I will be a mess, sometimes I will be restless, and sometimes I will be at peace. Knowing that these things cycle with the moon has made me feel empowered and able to let go, while also feeling more in control.

Charting Feelings

In this world of digital excess, there is nothing quite like a piece of paper in your hands. A real book, a real letter, a printed calendar that you can call your own. Let's explore the magic of getting out of the matrix and into the old ways of pen and ink and paper.

On the next new moon, use a page in your journal to chart your feelings each day for a week (or as many days as you can) so that you can begin to familiarize yourself with the "New Moon You." Track anything you want—we go far beyond emotion. I like to track my physical feelings, my energy levels, eating habits, and how easy things feel. I pay close attention especially to my skin and my general sense of well-being. What else seems important to you? Write it down. This practice will teach you more than you ever thought you could know.

WAXING MOON: GATHERING STRENGTH

What exactly is the waxing moon? For a long time I've been wrapping my head around this very question. "Waxing" essentially means "getting stronger." This is the phase after the new moon when the moon is growing. She's shifting from nothing, to that beautiful sliver and then she'll be full, before we know it.

During a waxing moon, we look for her reflection in ourselves, and we can use the waxing moon as a metaphor for our body and spirit. After the week of the new moon, things begin to grow and take shape. Perhaps dreams materialize or visions are clearer. Lisa Lister writes, "When the moon is 'waxing', it is getting larger in the sky, moving from the new moon toward the full moon. This is the time to start new projects, meet new people, conceptualize ideas and attract new love. The waxing moon phase lasts about 14 days."

Just as we did with the new moon, keep a journal. Each day, make your notes, and you will begin to see emerges in the sky of your being.

I feel much different on the new moon than on the full moon, and so the space between them is constant transformation; every day is different. In nature, a seed goes through so much just to sprout its little head up through the earth. Likewise, the waxing moon has a subtle transformation that is powerful nonetheless. A keyword for this phase is **gathering**. Gathering strength, gathering light, gathering shape, gathering gravity. The moon is gathering right now as she heads to fullness. What are you gathering? What is gathering around you?

Be open and receptive to what is coming through now. It doesn't have to be what you think it will be. What do you want? What tastes good right now? These are important things. Remember, keep it in the realm of easefulness. If you want to go on a vision quest, do it, but if not, that's fine too.

Perhaps the waxing moon phase is a time that you feel aligned with the pattern of growing stronger. Or maybe you don't feel that way, and so you look to the moon for help and support. She provides unmoving structure without the burden of rigidity. The moon says, "Follow me, but follow your heart also."

Gathering & Growing During the Waxing Moon

Because the waxing moon is often a time for gathering and growing, here are some extra ideas to incorporate twaxing time and use it to your benefit.

GATHER

Set aside some special time this week to head to your local market, co-op, or grocery store and gather what you need. Be intentional about it. Before you head out, check in with your heart's desires to see what nutrients your body needs.

If your body is on the same page as the moon, she's gathering strength, too, so rich and colorful foods or nourishing breads could be good right now. Only your body really knows.

COLLECT

Take a nature walk this week in your local environment, or one nearby. Perhaps this is a good time to visit the ocean or the mountains, or a park in your neighborhood will work. If you have children, bring them! Bring a basket or bag to collect natural treasures (sticks, stones, shells, feathers, leaves, flowers, etc.) that show up along the way.

BUILD

Use this week to build on a project you've already begun, or to start one you've been thinking about. Pull out the materials you need, or go buy the ones you've been putting off. Use the moon's energy to help you make some much-needed progress.

FULL MOON: FULL POWER

Full she rises in all her splendor. Many of us are aware of the full moon. Of all the phases, it is this one that has made it into pop culture, literature, and modern and ancient lore. The full moon is bright, visible and strong—often she keeps me (and many of you) awake much later than I'd like. The full moon is a time of peak fertility, literally and metaphorically.

The full moon brings a particular magic to all things. Whether it's artwork, a relationship issue, a vision being manifested, whatever it is, the full moon will lend power to it. It's helpful to set reminders for yourself during this time that your power source is turned up and you can accomplish many things!

If you feel like you need to be quiet and restful during the full moon rather than wild and full, then that's what you need. Write it down. Keep track. Notice. Listen. Your body speaks the truth, and your body communicates with the moon. The moon is different for everyone. And to be honest, such powerful energy can be completely exhausting, making the full moon a tender and sensitive time for people.

Remember, you can't do everything. Let yourself be you and let your needs be heard. For instance, there's a Kundalini training specifically about the moon that I have wanted to take, but I had to get real with myself and realize that now is not the time. I looked at what would suffer if I added that to my load, and I realized what would suffer is me.

So I chose to let go.

Like Yogi Bhajan says, we have enough information. What we need now is wisdom. Let us seek wisdom above all else.

To truly illuminate what the full moon personally means for you, I encourage you to write, write, write. Writing will help you find patterns that otherwise you might not pay attention to. You don't have to be like anyone else or like everyone else.

None of that is real anyway. Be yourself. Give it up to the moon, and let her lead you.

Letting Go

What are you willing to release that's not serving you? Do you have limiting ideas about the full moon that don't actually work for you? This is the perfect time to allow yourself to ditch those beliefs and create new ones of your own. I tend to be the kind of person who could eat the same thing every day for months. When I enjoy something, I want to do it every week (this drives my family crazy). My nature is to want things I can count on. I like structure. In maturing and finding personal freedom I let go of rigidity and open up to the flow. Meditating every day helps me be flexible within my need for structure.

Where are you rigid? Structure doesn't have to be rigid. This full moon, let yourself and others off the hook. Support people in ways that are easeful and obvious. Let your body tell you what ease means.

Write your full moon feelings down in your journal and track relevant feelings and patterns. Are you energized or exhausted? Are you feeling full and fertile, or delicate and quiet? Wherever you are, use the power of the moon to help you get what you need and allow it to validate your feelings and your truth.

EXTRA

The moon is at her biggest and brightest in this phase. If you can, go outside every night and look up at her for a little bit. This brief moment of connection will allow your body to align further with the moon and to soak up a bit more of that vibrant energy.

WANING MOON: REST & RETREAT

My relationship with the moon began when I had my first child. Each night I went outside with my babe in my arms and gazed at the moon. I sang, "I see the moon and the moon sees me. God bless the moon and God bless me" as I rocked him outside underneath the sky. My relationship began there because of the expanded state I was in as a new mother and also because that was the first time I began gazing at the moon with some kind of consistency. It all expanded from there … the moon began to help ease my mind and heart and I began to rely on her for her consistency and her change — such graceful balance. Developing this relationship with the moon made me realize that there's a cycle to everything — my mood, my emotions, my energy, my sorrow, my joy. This realization was liberating. It changed my life.

The waning moon cycle is like the sigh of relief after the full moon. The archetype associated with this phase is the Wise Woman, the woman who no longer cycles but has moved onto the esteemed realm of elders. There are many metaphors for this phase, and if any metaphors pop into your mind or heart right now, write them down so that you can learn from them. The waning moon can also be viewed as the "Autumn" of a moon cycle: the phase is coming to a close, winding down. Like trees in autumn drop their leaves, the waning moon allows us to shake off any leftover dead stuff that we may be clinging to.

Waning means the moon is getting smaller. Each os us need time like this, where we choose not to shine, where we choose not to reflect or stand out or sing to the world. We need times where we retreat and rest, withdraw into the quiet comfort of ourselves and leave everything else behind. We need to shed what doesn't serve us or what holds us back. Just as each day has a sunset and each month has a waning moon, we as women have our own period of retreat. Our own personal golden hour.

No woman can be her best without enough rest—we know this!

As this waning moon fades to black, I wish all of you the opportunity to rest in your cave of renewal and regeneration. Allow yourself to receive the unique gifts the moon is offering you and your beautiful body.

Cultivating Tranquility

Soothe

Choose 1-2 rituals this week to honor your body and cultivate peace in your cells. My go-to is always a hot bath, with or without essential oils. You can also massage your own feet at bedtime—this is a powerful self-love practice. Other ideas? Create your own!

Breathe

Increase your breathwork this week. In addition to your meditation practice, take 3 minutes each day to sit and focus on breathing deeply and oxygenating your body and blood. You can do this sitting up in your meditation space, laying in bed before you fall asleep, or even in the car in between errands. Increasing your attention to breath helps you remain open and expansive.

Bedtime

Honor your bedtime this week. Make it a real event. Set a time you want to be in bed by, and work backward from that point. What time will dinner need to be? How about that bath? Communicate this to your loved ones so that they can respect it. Wash your favorite pajamas and clear off your bedside table so that it is clean and peaceful. Wash your sheets, spray them with lavender water, and rest well.

Moon phase reflections

Use this space to take phase notes.

New //

Waxing //

Full //

Waning //

By paying closer attention to the moon this month, what did you learn about yourself? About your moods and cycles?

✎ ...

Journal

Journal

VENUS + GOLD

VENUS + GOLD

Goddess::
Pleasure and beauty,
a single flower in a mason jar.
Coconut oil all over my body before a shower.
Washing my feet before bed.
Listening to music with lights low as I brush my
teeth.
My favorite essential oil on my pillow.
An old silk dress that's holding on by a thread but
makes me feel gorgeous.

I choose you, Goddess
I see you all around me
I choose you by accepting myself and letting go of
limitation.
The Goddess is me.
She is you.
She is in the drink I made last night.
She is in the quiet of the night when I forget who I
am and then find myself all over again.

I am not afraid of getting lost anymore because I
know that whatever I will find will be truer than
before.
I don't need anything or anyone to validate me.
But if I listen carefully, the world I want is
whispering words of true encouragement into my ear.
(The world I do not want is telling me I'm not doing
it right).

```
I choose the world I want::
I choose me.

I choose.

I choose.

I choose.
```

PREGNANT WITH ALL THAT IS POSSIBLE

Goddess—the archetype, the energy, the myth, the creature. Who is she? Who is this all-encompassing Goddess about whom we hear so much? How do we find out who she truly is? How can work with her?

First let's note that the Goddess doesn't look any certain way. She's not always wearing a flowy dress nor does she always have long locks of hair. Women who embody the true Goddess source can show up in so many ways. We often associate Goddess energy with a certain way of looking or acting, but in truth the real Goddess shows up in women's ways of BEING. The Goddess knows no boundaries and she is not restricted by trends or styles. She simply IS.

The Goddess lives in you. This believing and knowing is available to all women. **Remember to never compare your insides with someone else's outsides.**

Who/what Goddess is for me will be different than who/what Goddess is for you. In fact, as I was writing thsis, it became so clear to me how we look to our teachers for guidance, yet our own process and truth will always be different than the process and truth of even our most beloved teachers. That can be tough to reconcile. We want to be led, but we must rely on ourselves

This is the call to courage. We must own our knowledge. We must own our power and intuition. We can look around us for inspiration, but the true knowing only comes from ourselves.

Goddess is not a person, a trend, or a look. She is many people, women, maiden mother and queen and crone. She is a feeling, a remeberance, she is kindness and fierce strength, she is saying NO even when others want us to say YES. She is saying YES when we know it's right. She is wisdom and truth, that feeling in our gut when we know what is right. She is Mother Earth, the water and the trees, the oceans and rivers, the beds in which we plant our gardens.

Look in your life for what aligns you with your true YES, the one that makes your heart sing. Maybe your Goddess shows up in jeans and a sweater, pants and a blouse; maybe she has green juice in hand or maybe it's a milkshake. Only YOU know.

Goddess mythology and history/story is abundant. We could spend years looking at this alone. Perhaps some of you identify with a particular Goddess from your childhood. If you've heard certain stories or myths as a young girl, maybe the legacy of those tales has stayed with you. In Western culture, we learn a lot about Greek mythology and the many golden-haired Goddesses who ruled the skies, the hearts of men, wisdom and wars. Goddess mythology goes so far beyond that. There are the Celtic Goddesses, Hindu and Indian Goddesses, Roman Goddesses, Egyptian Goddesses—and so many more that I don't even know about. Goddess myth is timeless, and it stays with us today.

Unleash Joy

Brainstorm. Write down all the words that come to you when you think "Goddess." Names are good, too. You can write down heroines, friends, mothers, people you know, anyone who reminds you of the universal Goddess.

If you have colored pencils or pens, add some color to your page—you can write the words in different colors, or add drawings that evoke the Goddess. Get as creative as you want, and make a beautiful page of Goddess brainstorm that you can look at any time you need to be inspired. This is a very fun project to do in groups or with friends. As an added dimension, you can do it in collage form as well to create a sort of Goddess vision board for your own Goddess truth.

Goddes Totems

Goddess totems don't have to only be actual Goddesses from Goddess myths. There are Goddesses in your lineage, Goddesses in your circle of friends. Many women in stories embody the Goddess, storytelling itself is a huge part of passing along Goddess traits and mentality. Trinity in the Matrix embodied Goddess energy—she was a warrior, but she was also a nurturer. This is part of the unique feminine power. Goddess is not always earthy and ancient. Goddess is always moving, she is adaptable, she shows up everywhere.

Explore your memory and your heart. Do you have any Goddess totems who already are with you? Perhaps she has been with you since childhood, or perhaps she has recently come to you. Did you read about her? How did you hear about her? Where did she first enter your consciousness?

Write her name at the top of a new piece of paper. Learn as much about her as you can. Start with a good old fashioned Google search. Ask around.

See if you can find books or movies about her. See where she shows up for you and surprises you.

DIVINE MYSTERY

What if throughout your day you bowed to the Goddess...bowed to yourself... humbly and with grace and with fierce devotion of self? What if when things were tough, you knew that—like the moon—things would find their way back, new and even deeper?

There's divine wisdom within women. It is one of the things we all have equal access to in this life. Many of us have strayed from our divine wisdom. We don't trust ourselves We see other women doing things, and we doubt ourselves and think, "She knows better", or the opporsite we judge the way she is doing it and think, "I know better."

What if we all just settled into ourselves for the answers, grace and wisdom that lives within us, and reached out to support, uplift and to listen? What if we leaned on the women who nourish us to listen to us and hold us up? What if we offered an arm to hold up the women we love?

Holy wow.
This is the revolution, women.
We cannot be bought or sold.
We are power full.

The divine mystery of woman and Goddess is revealed in many ways. Gathering and supporting one another is one of the ways in which this particular magic is unlocked and magnified. We must gather. We must support. We must create.

Another part of unlocking the divine mystery is embracing ourselves. This means loving the dark and the light.

Somewhere in that beautiful mess is our Goddess center, the truth of our being, the port of access to all divine feminine that transcends space and time. Turns out we don't need anything, really. It's all right there, inside of us.

Finding the Goddess Within

At the top of the page, write your own name. Then below your name, do a free-write brainstorm and write down anything about yourself that reminds you of Goddess. You will have to step outside yourself for this one. Pretend you are an onlooker, and let it flow Compliment yourself. Lift yourself up. Highlight your strengths. Just go for it. At the end, the paper will show you just how much you embody that perhaps you never even saw before.

NOURISHMENT AND THE FACETS OF GODDESS

I recently listened to a lecture by Yogi Bhajan. In it, he is sitting in the studio where I took my teacher training, where my beloved teacher Guru Singh teaches. The lecture is filled with gold. He says, *"When you practice kundalini yoga, you know who you are, and when you know who you are, you can't be controlled."*

I was reminded of this when I visited Glastonbury once, a mystical place that is filled with magic and deep wisdom. It's also filled with selling Goddess imagery.

I love to see art made in her image, but it made me think "The Goddess is not for sale." No one holds the key to Her. She lives within me. She lives within you. Within your mother and the woman who works at the grocery store. We all have Her within us, and we have Kali and Annapurna and all the facets of Goddess in each and every one of us.

We inspire ourselves by placing images and poems and stories by our bedside. We create altars to remember Her. We keep up with our practice so that we remember who we are.

I don't hold any of it for you. But I hold my hand out and give yours a squeeze. And I nudge you into the direction of your truth, of your soul, of you, because women have done it for me. And it's important that we do it for each other. This is how we nourish. We nourish ourselves, we nourish each other, we nourish the Goddess, we nourish the earth.

Rejuvenate Your Altar

This is the perfect time to revisit your altar. Your altar is a living space and doesn't need to always stay the same. How has the Goddess information affected your altar? Do you feel called to shake it up a bit?

Love yourself up and let your altar help you do it.

We build our lives every day, one brick at a time.

Recipes

GODDESS SCRUB

This is a simple self-care recipe that you can in many ways to make it your own.

Find a clean jar and fill it (almost, not all the way) with sugar. You can use any kind of sugar you like, they all work. Pour oil over the sugar until it's saturated. Grapeseed oil is a good one to use, or olive oil if you don't mind the smell. If you have some essential oils, a few drops will work wonders. You can also add in a couple teaspoons of coffee grounds to make it smell amazing and to add an extra revitalizing element for the skin.

If you want to add dried herbs or flowers, please do so. You can also make this scrub with sea salt instead of sugar. Now, take it in the shower and lavish yourself with this new treat.

CARRIE-ANNE'S YOGI TEA

15 whole cloves

20 green cardamon pods crushed or split

20 black cardamon pods

3 cinnamon sticks

8 slices of fresh ginger.

8 cups of water

Bring the water to a boil. Add the herbs. Cover and boil gently for 20-30 minutes. You can add a black tea bag at the end for a few minutes if you like, but if it is near the evening I leave it out. Strain the tea, add milk of your choice — almond, dairy, etc., and honey or maple syrup to sweeten.

Journal

Journal

HOLDING
HOME

HOLDING HOME

I am home.
I embrace home within me.
I am in my home.
I create home wherever I go.

 ::I am home::

I hold myself as sacred.
I create a home that reflects my inner world by:

- Creating a simple and sincere altar
- Keeping soothing sounds in my home
- Making simple and nourishing food
- Taking a bath (with essential oils and epsom salts) as a sacred self-care ritual
- Reading books that inspire and uplift me
- Creating reminders throughout my house of the values that are important to me

Home is a place where others feel nourished. Home is a place where I feel nourished. My physical home and my body home are so I can feel nourished, not to impress others.

When we create cozy homes, we create a place where we can be our true selves, love to our whole capacity, and feel joy from the simplicity of a mug in our hands, food on the kitchen table, a rug on our floor.

Home is
Where the heart is.

Make room.

*Clear out what
doesn't serve you in
order to bring in the life
you truly want.*

SACRED HOME

My home is my oasis of healing and love. My kitchen serves as
my church, and my wood table is the altar of my family.
— Carrie-Anne Moss

The space where you start and end your day is where we settle into
what's happening for us, what we are facing, what we need to look at.

For me, the more that my home feels sacred and cozy, the more that
I can relax my nervous system so that it can be deeply nourished. My
teacher Paramatma Siri Sadhana told me that my job is to keep my
nervous system relaxed so that my heart can be open.

If we aren't careful, our nervous system can get easily fried on the day-
to-day vibration of rushing, technology, and cars. I'm becoming more
aware of this and as I increase my awareness, I increase my ability to
regulate it and protect myself.

How to relax? This is the vital question. Rest is a crucial nutrient in
our lives and in our days. Rest isn't just something we should do when
we are exhausted, but something that we really should do before we
hit that point. I love to create my home and space so that it is restful
by nature. In this way, heals me. It helps me breathe, open expand.

Home is so many things. There is the old saying, "Home is where the
heart is." For me now in my life, home is here, in my house with my
family. It is where I live with them, eat with them, sleep with them,
nourish them — and where they nourish me. Home is in the bed with

my daughter asleep next to me; it is in the dark hours before dawn when I awaken by myself and go to the kitchen for my sadhana before anyone else awakens. It is in the tea that my husband brews for me in the glass kettle on the stove.

In these walls, I am home. Each day I strive to make this place a sanctuary not only for my guests and my family, but for myself so that I can truly be myself and find my center.

Restful Home

Making sure that my home feels restful and nourishing is a really big priority for me. My kitchen table is important to me because it brings people together allowing us to share and connect.

I started a tradition where I write questions on index cards and put them under everyone's plates before dinner. Only two of my family members ended up liking it, but it was still fun. On the cards I wrote things like *What is your best memory? What is your best moment from summer?* Even though not everyone loved it, I'm still going to keep it up for a while to contribute to dinner conversation (which gets more challenging as kids get older).

If you're single or don't have kids, you can still do this, or a version of it. You can still create questions or ideas and put them on cards under your plate! You could make a writing prompt, or even use oracle cards or tarot cards instead. Make up your own deck and then write every day in a time that is sacred … before breakfast, after dinner, whenever it is for you.

I want to encourage all of us to sit down for those meals, for that tea, with your journal and pen and look at it as a real opportunity to see what's going on with you. Let us embrace our eating spaces and our tables as holy, because they are. Let's allow them to nourish us, because that's what they do.

HAVEN

Haven (n): *a place where you are protected; a place that offers favorable conditions.*

When guests arrive at our home, they step into our entry way first. It is here that we exchange the first hug or the final goodbye, the greetings with loved ones or visitors from afar. It is the place of reception.

Often I walk into my home and the entry way is a mess. There are shoes everywhere, bags dumped on the ground, total chaos. I feel dread when I see this mess and I start up a story in my head about careless children and how no one helps out around here etc., etc.

Lately I have been able to transform that story into service: the straightening of the mess becomes a spiritual service. It is not just an offering to my family or messy children, but a meditative offering to myself, and an offering and honoring to my home. I believe there is a symbolism in each part of our house, and cleaning or embracing the entry way to my home lifes up the entry way into my heart as well.

I want my home to feel good for me, for my family, and for anyone who walks in that door. For me, that doesn't mean perfection—not at all. It doesn't mean immaculate furnishings or high style. For me it means deep love and raising the vibration. Making a home is an everyday exercise in these two things: deep love, raising the vibration.

There is a feeling we get when we come home — that feeling of "ahhhhhhhh." The sigh of arrival. The urge to change into something more comfortable. Sometimes there is the greeting from dogs, children, loved ones. There are the messes all around. The dirty dishes, the cluttered tables. These things exist in cycles without end.

But there is beauty in it. The beautiful mess of life reminds us that we are alive, that we have a bountiful existence, and that we have a home to hold us up.

Your Favorite Place

I love my kitchen table. It is my altar, my gathering place, and the space I truly love. Is there a place like this for you in your house?

Write in your journal about your favorite place in your home. It can be a whole room, or just a corner. Conjure the feelings that you have when you're in it, and write about why you love it. What aspects of this space speak to you? Does it heal you, nourish you, fill you up? Feel free to draw or collage as well, whatever inspires you most. Use your creation as a reminder of what makes you feel best when you create your space and your home.

RE-IGNITE, RE-INSPIRE, RECIPE

Let's face it: food is everywhere. There is no escaping the fact that we must feed ourselves morning, noon and night. Many of us not only feed ourselves, but our children and our families as well. Food is at the heart of it all and the kitchen is at the heart of our homes. The two cannot be separated, though I believe that the kitchen is about more than just food. It is about togetherness, creativity, joy and laughter, new thoughts and processing. It's about tea and ritual, dishes and messes, baking for birthdays and holidays.

Food is the ultimate offering and gift. When someone is over and you don't know each other that well yet—watch the whole experience transform as soon as you set out a plate of fruit and cheese, or crackers and pickles, or nuts and berries ... whatever you have on hand is enough.

We must create ritual from our food duties. This is how we can immerse in it and let it be wholly nourishing for us. If we can bring it in as a ritual of grace and view food as a communion with ourselves and those we love, then we are well on our way to deep happiness.

As women, we are hungry for connection and community. We long for gatherings of women and feelings of sisterhood. Nothing binds together a gathering, a circle, or a connection quite so much as sharing food. I think that over eons of history, it is food that has so often bound women and families together.

In our homes, we nourish ourselves in many ways. There is food, and there is rest; there is waking up each day to a new morning and to new possibilities. There is laughter late at night with people we love. Home is where we return to when we need to heal, when we are worn out, and when the rest of the world is too much to bear. There is so much nourishment in our homes. It's in our beds, in our cupboards of tea or medicine, in the fruit bowl on the counter. Keep our bodies and spirits, it all starts at home. And so much of it is held together by food.

If a child comes home grumpy and edgy, I gather my wits and remain as peaceful as possible, all while setting food out, quietly on the table. I won't say, "Eat this!" I just set it out so that he sees it. And soon enough, he eats it. And with each bite, the vibration changes. If a friend comes by needing support, I make tea right away. These offerings to our bellies sooth the heart.

Home is a beautiful space where we nourish ourselves. The board to cut on, the stove to simmer our soups, the oven where we bake, roast, and toast. Here is where we feed our bodies and in doing so, our hearts. And here is where, even unknowingly, we gather.

Gather Recipes

I love gathering recipes. How do you gather recipes? Do you have a box or a book that you add your own? Do you have a favorite cookbook, or do you always cook from the heart and head?

Gather recipes this week and find something new. A really fun way to do this is to ask a friend to send you a photo of her favorite recipe and you send one in return. A modern recipe swap. Or you can dig through books or Pinterest and find something that calls to you.

If there are others in your home, ask them if they have any new dishes in mind, or with children, you can look for recipes together to see what inspires the little ones.

Mung Beans & Rice

Yield: 8 servings

1 cup Mung beans

1 cup basmati rice

1 tsp. tumeric

9 cups of Water

8 cloves of garlic

1 heaping Tsp. Garam Masala

4-6 cups chopped Vegetables

Seeds of 5 Cardamom Pods

1/2 Cup of Ghee

1/2 tsp pepper

Salt or Soy Sauce. to taste.

1/3 Cup Chopped ginger root

Add rice and beans to boiling water. Cook for 45 min. or until soft. Add chopped vegetables in pot. Heat Ghee in skillet. Add Onions, ginger, and garlic. Saute until brown. Add tumeric, pepper, garam masala, cardamom seeds, and chiles. Cook 5 min. — Stir. Combine mixture with cooking beans and rice. Add soy sauce or salt. Serve with yogurt or grated cheese on top.

Recipe by Brian & Robyn Wolfe www.waldorfish.com

MAGIC & BEAUTY OF HOME

There's nothing in my home that is off limits; everything is meant to be touched and used. My couch is old and a little worn; we curl up in its corners and run fingers over our history that has woven itself into the fibers of each cushion. Our beds are covered with soft sheets that invite a deep and peaceful sleep. The table in my kitchen is beat up and scratched but I love it this way; every mark and dent holds a memory. I sit at one end and my beloved on the other. I have used the same chair for almost 8 years.

Homes are imperfect. Home is a story. We are part of it. Everything we own is a part of it. There is history, comfort, love, memory, nostalgia … anything you can think of, it's probably embedded somewhere in our home.

Home is about heart and connection and happiness, and about a space where we can feel safe to be ourselves and live our truth. It's about nourishing through food and through peaceful space. It's about creating joy by simply existing where we belong, and appreciating the view.

A FINAL NOTE

"Vibrate the cosmos and the cosmos shall clear the path."

You can change energy by putting music on. Music has a sound current which is a vibration.

I play Kundalini yoga music all the time in my kitchen. I love this music, but it also has an energetic purpose. The mantras have a vibration in sound and words. I pick the music that I need or my family needs. You may walk into my house and notice the music, but before long you stop noticing it and you just feel more relaxed because your parasympathetic nervous system is responding to the sound. Notice the music you play: How does it feel? How does it sound?

This week, bring music into your life where it might not be. Can you put it in your kitchen, or your bedroom? Does one of your children need some Kundalini music during homework hour?

WHAT I LEARNED FROM MY MOTHER

When I was young, my mother set the table each night for the next morning. She cleared the table and cleaned it, set out the plates, napkins and silverware before bed. As a child, I didn't think about it much. But now that I am an adult and a mother to my own children, it makes perfect sense, and I am once again awestruck at the brilliance of my own mother and what she was doing.

Adopting her practice, I now set the table before bed. I put out the essentials for our morning meal — mugs and spoons, bowls and napkins. I cannot overstate the deep satisfaction that comes from gazing upon a freshly-set table. This simple ritual changes the entire morning landscape for. Waking up and coming out to the kitchen to see this beautiful spread is heartwarming and rewarding. It brings me a very specific kind of joy, and all from my own hands. It is for me, for my family, for my children. We sit here and eat breakfast, drink tea, and laugh. We make a mess. The table, so perfect at first, will soon be filled with crumbs and dirty dishes and tiny handprints. This is all part of the beauty.

My own mother still does this, though we are all now big and grown. She said she began it as a way to help her when she was raising small children. It made the mornings easier, yes, but it also added an element of pleasure beyond just practicality. It brought beauty to her days.

Morning light shines in a different way than other light; it's a special gift that we receive each day if we are lucky. Setting the table at night helps to harvest the gift of morning light. It's like planting a seed, and in the morning you see the flower—the satisfaction is full and wondrous. This is a ritual, a practice to show devotion. I feel some kind of reverence as I incorporate this into my own life. Sometimes the best lessons are not ones that we learn in classrooms or in books, but in the subtle and quiet practices of our mothers and grandmothers.

Our homes contain so much of us. They house us and our families, but they also house the reflections of our hearts. Small rituals at home can have a big impact on our well-being. They let the light in.

There's a Japanese concept called Wabi-Sabi which essentially celebrates the beauty in imperfection and impermanence. This comes to mind for me when I think about setting the table at night. Part of the beauty is the way that the table looks when it's set. Everything is in order and the dishes are clean. When I wake up and look at it with the sunlight falling across it, I am moved by its loveliness.

There is something just as beautiful in making it messy. Breakfast is a special time; sitting at the table with my family in the morning is sacred. Mornings make me grateful. After breakfast, there is nothing left to do but to clear the table and take it all away. No more perfect place settings and pretty napkins—they're all a mess. But without the mess-makers, there would be no reason to set the table in the first place. Without one side, we cannot have the other. And so there is an inherent beauty in both.

Celebrate the beauty of imperfection and impermanence.

A Joyful Home

What are some things that bring joy to a home, a house? Start making a list so that when you are feeling like you need a joy boost, you can refer here and be inspired. We listed a few things to get you started. Remember, the possibilities are limitless:

Candles
Music
Cookies
Flowers
Clean Windows
Beautiful drapes…

What brings you joy?
 …

Heart of the home.

We mentioned this month that the kitchen is the heart of the home. How is your heart? How is your kitchen? What are some things you can do to nourish your heart through your kitchen?

Some ideas:

Make yourself a cup of tea

Stretch and open your heart center big and wide

Take a few moments to breathe

Put on music and do the dishes

Silence your phone and make a meal

Try doing your Sadhana in your kitchen…

What does your heart need? Your kitchen?

Expand.

✎ …

What is your greatest challenge in Holding your Home? Write about it here and brainstorm ways you can change it, even a tiny bit.

My challenge is:

✎ ...

Some changes to my approach could be:

✎ ...

Journal

Journal

RADIANCE
AWAKEN

RADIANCE AWAKEN

Dear Queen,

I see you in your strength and grace.
I see you move with poise and grit, with joy and
care.
I see you handling conflict with intellect and
intuition.
I feel you when you enter the room.

Your true beauty is your radiance pouring out of you
from within...
Acceptance of self is the portal into your radiance.
Looking like the standard idea of beauty is not real.
You are real.
You are radiant.
You are beautiful.

I am a woman.
Infinitely creative.

I am always changing.
Like the leaves that
change color,
I too have seasons
of my own,
and this is art.

THE RADIANT BODY

Kundalini yoga looks beyond the physical body. We are so much more than that in Kundalini yoga. We have ten bodies, and regular a kundalini yoga practice helps to balance these ten bodies. The tenth body is the what we call the Radiant Body. What is the Radiant Body? The Radiant Body is an energy field that extends nine feet around your body. Your crown chakra is where the energy comes in, and it moves through your spine and radiates outward, surrounding your aura. It can be viewed as a luminous outer layer of your aura, a golden crust.

It is this tenth body that brings you an air of royalty and grace; or of courage, confidence, certainty and generosity. When we think of someone who has poise or a powerful presence when they come in the room, these are the people working with a strong Radiant Body.

Yogi Bhajan said every woman is beautiful. I believe it. We are all so beautiful. Radiance comes from the inside, and when we cultivate it, it grows and shines. As we strengthen our heart center, beauty radiates more freely and easily.

How do we strengthen our heart energy? How do we waste our energy?

By:
Complaining
Competing
Comparing

An excellent practice is to abstain from these actions. My teacher Paramatma Siri Sadhana inspired this for me. She says that this may be the most difficult practice you will ever do. It takes discipline and grace, but just imagine what you will focus on when you take your energy away these wasteful, habitual actions. Radiance and joy will lift up from the corners of your being.

Instead of complaining, look instead to see what is working. Nurture what is good. Instead of comparing yourself to anyone else, connect to yourself. Ask yourself what you need. Connect to your truth and your soul and let those things be soft, let them shine. Know that you can never know truly what someone else's life is like. Comparing is a distraction from living your own life to its fullest. If you need to, take a break from social media so that you are not tempted to compare. Watch and see what happens as you recalibrate.

Comparing yourself is a distraction from living your own life to its fullest.

No Complaining

Let go of complaining, comparing and competing. Make this your practice today. Think of it in the morning when you first wake up. This practice takes attention, dedication, and discipline. Notice how it makes you feel. This will be very hard, but remember it is part of your sadhana practice. We are practicing and transforming.

When I say, "No complaining," I don't mean to stand by and be silent. I don't mean for you to settle for what is not right, or to be quiet if there is a wrongdoing at play. By not complaining, I mean for us all to bring constructive action to our lives. Complaining only points out what's wrong, but action creates movement and shift. If things need to change, it is up to each one of us to be part of that change in our personal lives and in the world. I do not suggest passivity—to the contrary—I suggest conscious awareness and empowered action. I suggest we use our creative energies for transformation, not for wishing things were different. The power lies in each of us, and each time we complain, we chose not to use our power.

When complaining is our practice, we block ourselves from action.

When we remove complaining, we remove the blocks.

THE BOWING BODY

By anchoring into the heart, we expand our vibration and exude through the Radiant Body to attract what we love.

The Radiant Body (in street talk it could be called *charisma*) is for us all. Everyone has access to it on the inside. The Radiant Body is subtle and doesn't come in the form of *Hey, look at me*! Rather, it comes in the form of a beautiful smile or a giving act, groundedness in your body. It comes in generosity and boundaries, it comes in being well-rested, certain and clear. It comes in joy and sadness, it comes in communication, and it comes in knowing who you are and standing unwavering in that truth. It comes in compassion and love.

Bowing
Every morning I bow. After I tune in with Ong Namo Guru Dev Namo, I bow. This is part of my morning practice, my sadhana. It creates fluidity and lubrication to my spine which I know is important for vitality and health.

Here is what else I receive when I bow:

I feel like a queen.
I feel like an empress and a mystic.
I feel elegant and full of the majestic.
I feel my lineage and the lineage of all the women who have come before me.

In five minutes of sitting on my knees and bowing in sets of four I get all of that. The bowing puts me in a state of gratitude. I bow. Yes I bow. I lay it all down in the morning. I humble myself. I honor myself. I wrap myself in a shawl and when I meditate I cover my head with it in reverence for the majestic beauty fully radiant queen that I am. I do it every single day because it matters so much to me. What started in discipline is now anchored in devotion. Devotion to myself, to my well being, to my radiance. I want to be radiant not to BE pretty or attract attention but to be truly beauty-full from within and to attract what I need.

As we continue to explore radiance, I bow to you. I see your beauty and your grace.

I bow to you.

I bow to your struggles and your pain.
I bow to your desires and your hopes and the love I know each of you feels deep within your soul.
I bow to this day.
To this moment.
To this breath to all that grows through all of us.

Bowing

As you go through your life, can you find it in you to bow to your beauty and radiance, to your love and life? Imagine what kind of choices you would make.

Throughout your day, energetically bow. With an inner awareness, bow.

In the pain and sadness, bow.

In the frustration, bow.

In the joy, bow.

This is an inner act. You can also do it physically whenever you feel it. Bowing puts you in your heart.

:: I BOW TO YOU ::

RADIANCE IN THE WORLD

I saw a woman at the grocery store recently when I was doing my shopping. This woman was so beautiful to me. Her face was lined by life and years and lit by an inner glow. I was deeply taken by her radiance; it washed over me with such clarity that **this** is the beauty I want to emanate. True radiance, glowing from a life well-earned. Lit from within.

I know I was only catching a glimpse of this radiant woman, but what I saw moved something inside of me. Her real beauty, her authenticity, and her courage radiated from her very presence.

Finding your authentic voice in your day-to-day life can take a lot of filtering. For me it also takes protection. Protection from a society that makes very little sense to me. A society that doesn't value mothers or aging. A world that, if we let it, will turn us against ourselves.

This is where the **fierce** me comes in. I won't become a victim of this paradigm. Instead, I will create and nurture in myself what an authentic woman is to me. I will choose how I live my life; I will create the world I long for. I will not place blame. I will empower myself with the knowledge that it all comes from within. I will let go of my ideas for how things *should* be, and I will bravely stand in the unknown.

Radiance in Ourselves

As I sit at the altar of my soul, I know that being authentic is important to me. When I carve out time to sit quietly and breathe, stretch, and bring myself back to the center of my being, I find my life works better. I find it easier to live in the radiance I crave. I find the ease to illuminate.

In the space of this daily ritual I connect to myself and when I do, these are some of the benefits I have witnessed in my life:

- I forgive myself and others.
- I have more patience.
- I trust myself.
- I love and cherish my body, respect it, and nourish it.
- I feel more creative.
- I sleep well.
- I let go of what I think I know.
- I transform my fear around aging and find the beauty in this time
- of my life.
- I strengthen my core so that I can unleash my creativity and feel the power of my center.
- I notice others who emanate strength and radiance.
- I love myself with all my imperfections.
- I dance and sing, tuning into my heart and my sensuality, raising my vibration.
- I laugh.
- I surrender it all.

In finding my authenticity, I craft my life in a way that resonates with my values and my truth. As women we must come together and lift each other up to be in our natural radiance. We have so much power.

Through our meditation practice, we are able to anchor ourselves and not be run by the unconscious mind.

Many of us might not even know the subtle things we do to sabotage what we want. Do you spend endless amounts of time on social media or surfing the web when you could put discipline time into connecting to yourself and creating what you want? It's hard sometimes connecting to yourself and allowing your creativity to really flow.

*Create the space
to download
your creativity.*

I recommend that every day we create space by meditating or unplugging. In meditation we bow to the divine wisdom that lives within us and all the divine wisdom that's come before us, and that's a big deal.

It's a beautiful simple act.

You are the lighthouse.

Tend to Your Altar

If you don't have an altar, use this time to build one. If you have one, tend to it so that you can connect with yourself, with grace, and with your radiance. Tending to your altar means cleaning it, refreshing it, adding new things (or taking away old ones) and spending time with it.

STRENGTHENING THE BODY

As women, we must build our sacred circle. We must bolster our inner strength, fortify our container, and remember to not look outside for answers and validation.

It wasn't too long ago that if I felt stress, I instantly called a friend to have her tell me what to do. It is my distraction-meets-panic-mode. I felt it just the other day, and noticed quickly how far I've come. I don't need others to tell me how or what to do. I can sit uncomfortably knowing that it will pass and change (thank you, moon).

I have grit to keep up
Thank you Radiant Body Kriya
I have mental patience and clarity
Thank you Sat Ta Na Ma
I have faith in the way my life is unfolding
Thank you Aad Guray Namay

The Archer
Another way to strengthen the Radiant Body is through a Kundalini yoga pose called the Archer pose. The Archer pose is a warrior pose and it builds confidence and self-esteem; it is firmly rooted, heart is open, aim is true.

I love the Archer pose.

While the Archer pose appears in Kundalini Yoga, it is also a widespread archetype that appears in many stories throughout the world and through history. In Greek mythology, Artemis was the Goddess of the hunt and the protector of the animal kingdom; she was also the goddess of both virginity and childbirth, and she is associated with the moon. She is often pictured with a bow and arrow. The bow and arrow, the tool of the archer, is a metaphor for the particular strength of the tenth body. this means it is not just the weapon itself that is important, but it is the aim, and the clarity of intention that matter so much. Additionally, it is the careful drawing back of the string that determines where the arrow will fly. Pulling back the bow can only be done properly when we are rooted, clear, strong, and certain.

I know my worth. Sometimes I falter and forget, but I quickly work to reconnect myself. My beauty is that I am a woman. My connection to the wisdom I have within me holds me up, as do the walls in which I live. I have earned this grace. I have reprogrammed myself from being needy and insecure to knowing that I have all the wisdom I need.

Archer Pose

Practice The Archer pose and see what it brings to you. Try it for 3 minutes on each side as is suggested. Do this daily and tune in to how it makes you feel or any changes that you notice.

Visualize it

What do you feel your radiance LOOKS like?

Is it super bright? Is it light and airy? Is it smooth, or fuzzy, or pointy?

:::::

On the following page, use your medium of choice (colored pencils, water colors, crayons, etc) to create a visualization of your Radiant Body. Don't over think it, just feel it flow out of you.

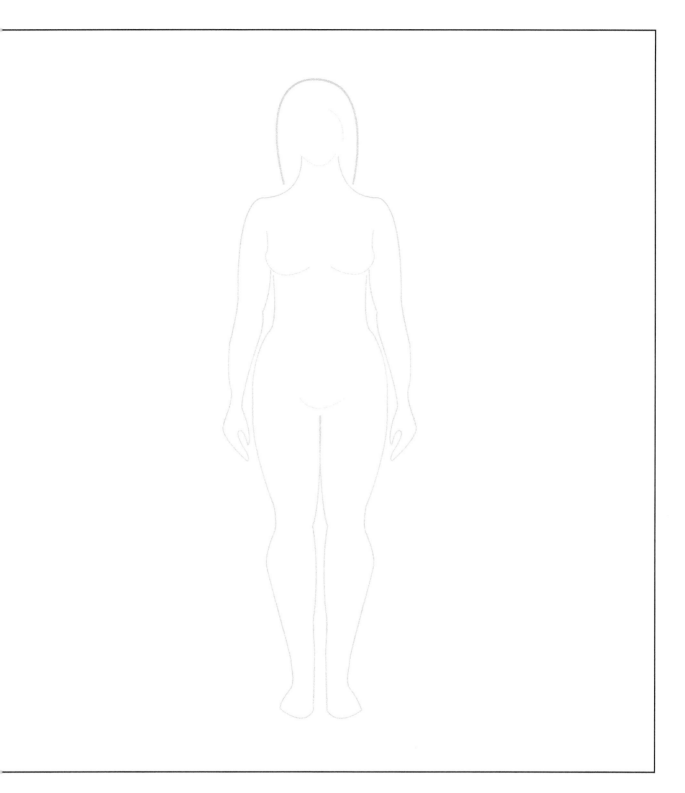

Journal

Journal

BY THE FIRE

BY THE FIRE

I'm soft, you see.
I walk out the back door of my house in the dark of
the morning to gather wood for the fire
I usually wear my slippers, but truth be told I can
do it barefoot because I live in California.
I'm soft and strong
I'm privileged and grateful.
I remember my childhood, and growing up the way I
did means I never take my life for granted.
I appreciate the smallest of things because it makes
me happy.
I feel grateful for the walk outside in the morning,
it sets the tone for my life.
Listen for what the morning sounds like,
what the sky looks like.
Where is the moon?
Oh there she is...
hi...

I get to start again and again.
I light the fire with simple reverence.
I feel like a Queen, but please don't take a picture,
because I most likely don't look like one in my
mismatched outfit and crazy hair (but I don't care).
I want to feel like the Queen.
I know what it takes to get the perfect picture and
that's not what I am going for.
I'm going for deep pleasure,
the kind that lives within me.

I'm going for Fierce Grace, and that, my friends, is
not for sale. This life is mine and I will live it
my way.

Live your one life
with your heart and your soul.

Light the fire.

THE FIRE WITHIN

More than ever, we must sing hallelujah.
We must rise up.

By leaning on our community, by giving to our communities, by using our Sadhana practice, and by standing in love, we can move through these times with more grace.

At this moment in time we are being called upon to be soft yet fierce. We are being asked to hold innocence but not naïveté. We are being asked to be Strong Women. More than ever, we must rise to these challenges. We must flow like water and be accepting, but we must have clear boundaries and know where the river bank lies.

Winter is a season for quiet strength and for going inward. The days grow shorter, nights are longer, and we approach the winter solstice — the longest night of the year. Though the darkness seems overwhelming sometimes, it's a great opportunity to get things done. In the longer days of summer, we are summoned away from our homes and our sanctuaries for play time and gatherings. In winter, we get opportunity for quietude. Use that opportunity to your advantage.

Here are my intentions this season:

My intentions start with simplicity. The simple truth of what it is I'm really craving right now. I'm craving joy and laughter, I'm craving lightness and depth. I'm craving community and connection, I'm craving authentic conversations and I'm craving true listening, myself as the listener and also in being heard. I want to be able to be with my children and my husband in new and expansive ways, in order know who they are. I want to be kind and patient and I want to make really delicious food. I want to be of service. I want to expand my heart and consciousness so that I understand how much I truly have to share and receive and to give. I want to listen to music 24 hours a day, even in my sleep. I want mantra! I want early morning Sadhana. Did I already say I want community? I want community, community, community. Simple and sincere community.

Write yours.

CHERISHED FAMILY

Where can I start? At home.

I ask you – can you be with your family in a new way? What do they need? What do you need? How can you use this season to your benefit?

For many people the holiday season brings up big stuff: Family pain, childhood sadness and a feeling of melancholy. I know that this is not an easy time for people who feel this way. As I've mentioned before, this season is the darkest hour the hour before the dawn, and this aspect (combined with holiday emotions) can be a lot to bear. Holidays are rife with memories and nostalgia and while some nostalgia can be sweet, much of it can be limiting. I've heard it said that nostalgia is just memory with the bad parts wiped away. Be gentle on yourself and others and remember there is no golden standard for this season. It will be what it is, and nothing is perfect.

I love this time of year. The early nights bring me inside more and winter brings creativity to the forefront of my days. It wasn't always like his for me. I often missed home. I missed my mother and all those incredible holiday memories from my childhood. I would often feel nostalgic for the big family gatherings at my grandmother's house, her apple pies and the talent show that my cousins and I would put on. I found myself cooking Christmas dinner with a feeling that the meal didn't taste as I remember it. Over time, however, I learned to let those memories live in a special place, sort of like an ornament on a tree: something to be admired and appreciated, but certainly not something to rule my days. My nostalgia is a wonderful part of the holidays for me, but I focus on creating the holidays that I want my children to remember. My nostalgia does nothing for them. It is only my actions and my choices that shape their memories.

NOURISMENT

The Winter Solstice is the darkest night of the year. This darkness opens doors to your heart and prayers, and intentions have extra potency. In all this silence and darkness, it is easy for gratitude to flow in all directions. As the solstice night approaches, consider what your prayers are and for whom: yourself, loved ones, the earth. Consider what you will leave behind for this next cycle around, the things that are heavy on your shoulders and your heart. Write them down if you wish.

Things I will do to simply celebrate the Winter Solstice:

- I will update my altar for Winter Solstice with images of Goddess and the sun.
- I will do a deep, simple clean of the house. I will declutter, wash all the blankets and refresh the essential oils in my diffuser.
- I will eat by candlelight at breakfast and dinner.

The Winter Solstice means we are going through a time of transition, we are pushing through the final layer of darkness and surfacing toward the light. In this journey there is growth, expansion, reaching, rooting.

- Can we look at ourselves in the eye and tell ourselves that we are loved?
- Can we wrap ourselves in soft blankets and turn off our phones?
- Can we make a simmering broth and feed it to ourselves each day?

The answer is YES.

What nourishes you? How about spaciousness ... a quality that is often lost to its opposite: the endless errands, the over-full schedule, the to-do list that won't quit, the constant notifications on our phones. To create spaciousness in this day and age takes effort. And you know what? It's worth it.

Radical self-care is about allowing yourself to be who you are so that your true love vibration can overflow and move outward, touching those around you. But first, you must love yourself. You must allow yourself the things you would allow your children: love, food, rest, laughter, play, snuggles...the list goes on. Think about how you care for your partner...this care is also what you deserve.

Spaciousness is a sweet beloved friend who restores us, brings peace to our hearts, and puts delight on the faces of our lovers and our children. Life can be stressful and people forget to create space. I encourage you to embrace spaciousness as a radical act right now. Prioritize it. Let it be part of your ritual, your tradition. Let it be known that you value it.

Last year, I wrote a letter to the Wintertime to tell it what I wanted. This helped me so much in knowing how I wanted to live the season and be with my family. Here is what I wrote:

Dear Winter,

I want to hear your voice. I want to understand and take the time to hear your message to my heart. I want to nourish myself in every moment through what I think and how I interact with my beloveds. As I light the fire in the morning I will make a wish into the fire. Today it will be for laughter. And when I light it at dinner, as I bring the wood in from outside I will connect with reverence like I am a woman who lived deep in the forest years ago and who needed this fire to keep warm to thrive.

I will respect you that much.

I will drink ginger tea with homemade almond milk as I sit next to you, my dear strong friend.
I will write a poem for you today and I will take a bath as if it were the sweetest thing I could ever do.

I will do this because this most precious life of mine is a gift and I want to celebrate the mundane with all the magic I can.

Love,
Carrie-Anne

*Love can be expressed
in words, but it is often
through actions
that it is truly felt.*

THE SPIRIT OF SERVICE

In our world of consumerism, service stands out. There are opportunities everywhere for us to give to those in need. I know a woman who, when she was a child, went with her mother to the local church and they pulled a child's name off of the tree. Then she would get to choose what to buy for this particular child, and wrap it, and bring it back to the church, which delivered the gifts to the children in need.

Where do we start? Which organization aligns with our own core values? Which organization is authentically giving most of the donations to the poor and hungry? Do we simply donate possessions, or do we want to volunteer for a kitchen and actively feed the hungry? These are all good questions that are best addressed within ourselves and within our communities. I encourage you to ask people close to you what they know about giving to those in need wherever you live. Local churches have great programs. You may be surprised what you learn.

While the spirit of giving should certainly encompass the poor, we don't need to confine it only to that. Everyone needs something. Everyone knows the astonishing joy and relief when we receive a random act of kindness. Kindness does not discriminate. It is valuable to everyone. Service is an act of love, and by acting in love, we engage in our highest selves, we activate our deep truths and we clear the way to living the life we love.

At this point in time, we must give to receive. Look around you. Where is your community? Who are they? Who is your support? Who is in need? Be aware of what you have to offer, and offer it whenever you can. Accept gifts and give freely. Love thy neighbor, and don't look too far for your tribe. See what is close to you and how you can use it to build a strong foundation for yourself and your family.

Below is a poem that inspires the spirit of service in me.

Dance

Cry

Kneel

Say thank you to all that you have experienced this past year

Get grateful

See what you do have

Kiss it all with your heart, and stretch to see what you truly desire

Feel it — here is magic in the air and it is there for you

We are the ones we've been waiting for.

Words for the Year

What are your two words for the year? Don't think too hard about it, let the words come from the heart as much as possible:

 ...

A Letter

Write a letter to winter. What do you want from it, how are you feeling, what do you have to offer?

 ...

Journal

Journal

I AM

I AM

I am who I am thank god I am.
I think this so many times a day.
I am grateful.
I am so grateful.

I have many tools that I lean on while navigating
these days, these months, these years.
I am who I am.
I am worthy.
I am true.
I am strong
and clear and grounded.

When I am grounded and strong and connected
I can do anything.
Grounded women cannot be manipulated.

I will never be perfect (thank god).
Perfection kept me small and afraid.
I will live my life following the sound of me.
The gift of this life is to be true.

May we collectively rise with hearts wide open
To be all that we gloriously are.

I am the light of my soul
I am beautiful
I am bountiful
I am bliss

I am, I am.

When I see nature mirror to me how I feel within, I remember the truth of who I am.

NOURISHING ALL OF ME

When I bring things to my life, I want them to stretch me, but hopefully not complicate my life. An example: one of my teachers offers incredible courses, and I take them and gain a lot from them. But I often end up feeling badly, because I just can't keep up. I get irritated when I can't watch the live videos, and then that stress comes out in my day-to-day interactions. So unless I can accept that I am not going to be able to do it all and get what I can from it without feeling stressed...then I just can't do it.

There is a time and a season for deep immersion, and right now—as a mother of three, a wife, a woman with a career, etc., **simple and sincere** works best for me. Sure, there are many incredible meditations, but a simple practice feeds me and doesn't take from me. It's a fine line where to stretch and where to say, "This is good enough."

As we move through life navigating all the bits and pieces of our unique and personal experiences, there is always opportunity to grow. Our lives are our classroom.

There will be days of ease and days of struggle and days of everything in between. With clarity and softness, strength and grit, we can ride the waves of our lives with grace and joy. Gone are the days of wishing things were different. Certainty starts within us in the depth of our soul and our connection to it.

Here is the definition of soul, according to Merriam-Webster:

- "The immaterial essence, animating principle, or actuating cause of an individual life
- The spiritual principle embodied in human beings, all rational and spiritual beings, or the universe
- A person's total self"

Nourishment must be a priority. We must be aware of what we feed our body, mind and soul. Acceptance of others is key, and the clarity to tend to our inner landscape can make all the difference in our lives. There is grief and loss, celebration and growth often in one day.

Here are some simple yogic tips that I love for dealing with a crisis situation (from Yogi Bhajan).

- When we are dealing with something intense and find ourselves needing to face it in the moment, drink a full glass of water.
- Don't sip—drink it in one breath. This will automatically calm you. It slows the breath, lowers the temperature; and a pause in the middle of a crisis can give you a clearer, more neutral perspective. It can make you part of the solution instead of the problem.
- Slow down the breath.

So much is attained by slowing down the breath. When I'm stressed I either hold my breath or start breathing rapidly. Inhale sat, exhale nam. Bringing attention to our breath is a godsend.

LOOKING BACK, LOOKING AHEAD

The end is truly the beginning. They are separated only by a hair. I invite you to look at the year ahead of you. Perhaps when you close your eyes, you picture yourself on the luminous precipice where past becomes future: the present.

Reflection is a keyword for you right now — look how far you've come! How did you grow last year? What did you learn? What will you leave behind, what burdens have you learned to let go?

As we move through life and become older, I like to think that we journey ever-closer to the center of our selves. We listen more to the whispers, we care less about what people think and we break the shackles of expectation, beauty norms and obligation. We find freedom in the simple and the mundane.

If you take a moment to look ahead, to dance in the possibility of creation and dreams, what do you see? What lies ahead for you?

Keywords for this season are home and security. Lift these themes up and away from obligation, bathe them in light and love. What remains when you do that?

In Fierce Grace
I lean on myself,
I gather my strength,
I learn to speak my
truth.

"I HAVE EVERYTHING I NEED"

We carry our gifts with us ever forward in our march. We bow when we need to; we pull out our cosmic bow and arrow when we need, pulling back strong toward the heart, and releasing with true aim.

If I could have only one wish for you, it would be that you walk forward with the gift of knowing that **you are enough**. Know that no one else knows what you know and there is no teacher who can give you the answers. You have the answers within yourself. You don't need me (or anyone) to give you what you need because it's already yours. When you take the time to connect with yourself, it's all there.

Connect to yourself with your daily practice (our sadhana). The more you practice it, the more you know yourself...and the answers. As we age and grow older, as we deepen our practice, we become liberated by knowing ourselves. This way we don't have to wait on people to reveal things and we don't give away our power by thinking someone else knows what we don't. No more time in bad relationships or in situations that harm us. Rather, we move with Clear Knowing because we know ourselves.

We all have the ability to create what we truly crave. No one will give us the life we yearn for; we have to claim it. So I ask myself, what do I want? What do I really want?

I want connection to my soul and connection to my husband. I want to laugh with my children and feel the joy bubbling up out of the freedom to play. I want deep conversations with my best women— each of them a goddess. I want to laugh 'til I cry with my sweet mama and to dance in the kitchen just because. I want to help the woman in the grocery store get her cart and feel that being of service is in the flow of my daily experience. I want to find the space daily to dive deep into my yoga practice and feel the ecstasy of my soul. I want to create art for fun.

I want to feel purposeful as I tend to the needs of my life. I want to notice the trees and the moon and the children who are finding their way. I want to feel compassion for the angry and the hardened, I want to give someone comfort in the way I see them and hold them with my energy.

Oh, blessed am I to ponder such things in a world with so much strife! Loving this life with its hard and rough bits, while truly holding gratitude through it all, is a challenge for me daily.

Love yourself. Don't wait for someone else to love you. Don't wait until you lose weight, find the love of your life, or get that dream job. The time is NOW, just as you are. You are enough. If you hold ANY story that gets in the way of you loving yourself, let it go. Rewrite your story.

ENDING NOTES

A few reminders:

- Share yourself.
- Find your tribe.
- Listen to your body.
- If being with someone depletes you, maybe it's time to take a break.
- Share your life with others who inspire and uplift you—and give it back to them.
- Be of service.
- Taking our attention off ourselves and giving it to others in need fills us up.

Create what you crave. Keep it simple. Create community. Host a yoga class in your living room. Take a thermos of tea to the park and bask in the luxury of nature. Whatever speaks to you—create it.

Start with small declarations of claiming this life. Put your favorite flower on your desk. Make your bed beautifully—a love letter to yourself. When you slip into your bed at night feel the loving intention this action creates for your body. Whisper *thank you* to yourself. Wear your favorite velvet dress around the house as you do your daily chores; don't save it for a special occasion. Make your life that special occasion. Be mindful of the ways you speak about yourself and your life.

Remember to check your altar. This is an important time to look at it, love it, breathe life into it, and bless it up with gifts, cleaning, however you see fit. Remember the moon, our protectress and compass, our anchor point. Going by the lunar calendar can be a challenge in Western society, but it can also be a luminous secret kept in one's pocket, lighting the way with it's quiet glow.

Gather & go

forth.

Journal

Journal

CREDITS & REFERENCES

Book credits:

Book design and layout by Loretta Neal. www.lorettaneal.com
Book editor Sadie Rose Casey. www.sadierosecasey.com

Photography credits:

Michelle Gardella for photography throughout the book. Used with permission from the photographer. www.michellegardella.com
Catherine Just for author photo. Used with permission from the photographer. www.catherinejust.com

Citations:

Guru Rattana, Ph.D. (1988) *Relax and Renew with the Kundalini Yoga and Meditations of Yogi Bhajan.* Sunbury, Pennsylvania: Yoga Technology, LLC.

Guru Rattana, Ph.D. (2014). *Transitions to a Heart Centered World.* Sunbury, Pennsylvania: Yoga Technology, LLC.

Artwork credits:

Cover painting by Rachael Rice. www.rachaelrice.com
Watercolor background on cover by Sneha Mohanty at Essem Creatives
Recipe by Brian & Robyn Wolfe www.waldorfish.com
Pencil icon by Edward Boatman from the Noun Project

Water color washes on prompt pages:

Created by Kjpargeter / Freepik.com

Designed by Harryarts / Freepik.com

Purchased fromw River and Tree / Etsy.com

CPSIA information can be obtained
at www.ICGtesting.com
Printed in the USA
BVHW022107150320
575088BV00014B/65